TRANSFORMED  LIFE

Practical, inspirational, and most of all, field tested and successful in one of the UK's most engaging churches, *Transformed Life* is a dynamic resource that points to this core truth: authentic discipleship leads not just to behavioural modification, but to character transformation through God's Spirit. Highly recommended.

– Jeff Lucas, speaker, author, and broadcaster

It is virtually impossible to enjoy the fullness of your Christian life without wholeheartedly embracing your new identity in Christ. Working through Paul's superb teaching on this theme in Ephesians 1–3, with the aid of such a fine pastor/teacher as Dave Smith, is an absolute winner! Let me urge you to take advantage of this excellent material.

– Terry Virgo, Founder of Newfrontiers

Dave Smith is one of the most inspirational Christian leaders in the UK today. Through this book we can learn much from his wise and penetrating reflections on the teachings of the New Testament and grow as followers of Jesus Christ.

– Nicky Gumbel, Vicar of HTB

If the book of Romans is the Himalayas of Bible peaks, then Ephesians is the Alps! Either way, we need wise guides to help us negotiate the wonders of Ephesians 1–3. Dave Smith has done a magnificent job to engage our minds, and hearts, so we can grasp profound and practical truths daily, and then climb higher.

– Greg Haslam, Senior Pastor of Westminster Chapel

Transformed Life is a great resource. It is more than a book; it is packed with scriptural life-building materials suitable for personal devotion and in-depth study. I loved the memory verses and concluding faith declarations designed to earth the truth and bring life-transforming impact.

– Stuart Bell, Senior Pastor of Alive Church and Leader of the Ground Level Network

TRANSFORMED  LIFE

Discovering our identity,
belonging and purpose
Ephesians 1–3

DAVE
SMITH

Acknowledgements

I would like to say a special thanks to a few people; to J.John for his thorough and insightful feedback, and to my wife Karen for her detailed proofread of the original manuscript and for her loyal love over the last nearly 30 years of marriage. Thanks also to Tom Webster for his help with some of the original illustrations.

Finally, a big thanks once again to the amazing church family at KingsGate. It's great to be on the journey together.

Copyright © 2015 Dave Smith
Published 2015 by CWR, Waverley Abbey House, Waverley Lane, Farnham, Surrey GU9 8EP, UK.
CWR is a Registered Charity – Number 294387 and a Limited Company registered in England
– Registration Number 1990308.
The right of Dave Smith to be identified as the author of this work has been asserted by him in
accordance with the Copyright, Designs and Patents Act 1988; sections 77 and 78.

For list of National Distributors, visit www.cwr.org.uk/distributors
Unless otherwise indicated, all Scripture references are from the Holy Bible, New International
Version Anglicised (NIV) copyright © 1979, 1984, 2011 by Biblica (formerly International Bible
Society). Used by permission of Hodder & Stoughton Publishers, an Hachette UK company. All
rights reserved. 'NIV' is a registered trademark of Biblica (formerly International Bible Society).
UK trademark number 1448790. Other Scripture quotations are marked: Amplified: Scripture
quotations taken from the Amplified® Bible, copyright © 1954, 1958, 1962, 1964, 1965,
1987 by The Lockman Foundation. Used by permission. ESV: Scripture quotations are from
the Holy Bible, English Standard Version, published by HarperCollins Publishers © 2001 by
Crossway Bibles, a division of Good News Publishers. Used by permission. All rights reserved.
NLT: Scripture quotations marked (NLT) are taken from the Holy Bible, New Living Translation,
copyright © 1996, 2004, 2007 by Tyndale House Foundation. Used by permission of Tyndale
House Publishers, Inc., Carol Stream, Illinois 60188. All rights reserved. NRSV: the Scripture
quotations herein are from the New Revised Standard Version Bible, copyright © 1989, by
the Division of Christian Education of the National Council of the Churches of Christ in the
U.S.A., and are used by permission. All rights reserved. *The Message*: Scripture taken from
THE MESSAGE copyright © 1993, 1994, 1995, 1996, 2000, 2001, 2002. Used by permission
of NavPress Publishing Group.
Every effort has been made to ensure that this book contains the correct permissions and
references, but if anything has been inadvertently overlooked, the publisher will be pleased to
make the necessary arrangements at the first opportunity. Please contact the publisher directly.
Copy adapted from *Five Hundred Gospel Sermon Illustrations* © copyright 1987 by John Ritchie.
Published by Kregel Publications, Grand Rapids, MI. Used by permission of the publisher. All
rights reserved.
Their Finest Hour reproduced with permission of Curtis Brown, London on behalf of the Estate
of Winston S. Churchill. Copyright © The Estate of Winston S. Churchill.
Concept development, editing, design and production by CWR
Cover image: OneDollarPhotoClub/ Jag_cz
Printed in the UK by The Linney Group
ISBN: 978-1-78259-412-3

Contents

Foreword

If you were to carry out a popularity poll on the books of the New Testament, the top three would almost certainly be John's Gospel and the letters to the Romans and the Ephesians, and I wouldn't be at all surprised if Ephesians made it to number one. While remaining accessible throughout, there is nevertheless something majestic and breathtaking about the range and depth of the letter to the Ephesians. It is a book rich in truth and insight, and it is hard to read more than a couple of verses without being blessed by some wonderful and striking idea. Ephesians is a letter that every Christian should read regularly: trust me, neither you nor I are going to fully grasp everything in it this side of eternity. For depth, breadth and sheer spiritual impact there is nothing to touch it in the New Testament.

There are three aspects of Ephesians that particularly strike me.

The first is that Ephesians is **enlightening**. In one sense, the good news of the gospel is very simple: those who trust in Jesus are forgiven by God, because at the cross He paid for our sins. Yet that wonderful truth is just the central mountain peak of an endlessly vast landscape that cries out to be explored. Why did God save us? What are we saved for? Where is Jesus now and what is He doing? Why do we face opposition in the Christian life? The answers – or at least some of them – are given here in this extraordinary letter. Ephesians sheds light on some of our deepest questions.

The second is that Ephesians is **encouraging**. For a lot of people, for a lot of the time, life is like walking through treacle. The toxic philosophy we live and breathe on a daily basis tells us that life has no purpose and no ultimate meaning. Someone has said, 'Life is like an onion: you peel off layer after layer and then you find there is nothing in it.' Ephesians is a wonderful antidote to that attitude of gloom. It offers a majestic, awe-inspiring view of existence for the Christian. We have meaning, we have purpose and we have a future that is glorious beyond words. For example, let's pull out one little phrase: 'For we are God's handiwork, created in Christ Jesus to do good works' (Eph. 2:10).

Think about those words and how they apply to you, and let those thoughts change your life.

Finally, Ephesians is **exciting**. To read anything of the history of the Early Church, or of those times when God has moved in power, is to encounter men and women who have been excited by what God has done. Nothing communicates more strongly than excitement! And there is probably no book in the New Testament more exciting than the letter to the Ephesians. Every line seems to contain a new, striking and challenging truth. For example, over thirty times in this letter Paul describes believers as being '*in* Christ' – a tiny but powerful reminder that we are risen with Christ and linked eternally with Him. And in an age when many people struggle with the idea of church, Ephesians speaks of the Church as God's building (2:19–22), Christ's Body (1:23; 4:16; 5:23) and His bride (5:25–27). It's an exhilarating and life-changing perspective on how we should view our fellowships. Reading Ephesians thoughtfully should always move us to excited prayer and praise.

Thank you, my friend Dave Smith, for helping us to study Ephesians, and to understand and apply its truths to our lives, so that our lives can be transformed. I was certainly enlightened, encouraged and excited when I read and studied the manuscript.

Rev Canon J.John

Introduction

Welcome to *Transformed Life*! I am so excited that you have decided to join us on this spiritual journey, as we examine three of life's most important questions:

Who am I?   Where do I belong?   What am I living for?

These questions of **identity**, **belonging** and **purpose** are vital for our whole existence and security. Sadly, many people spend much of their lives confused concerning their true identity, place of belonging and real life purpose – a bit like in the story of the ugly duckling. Let me summarise for you:

A young bird was born into a family of ducks, only to be verbally and physically abused and rejected, because he was ugly, and clearly didn't look like or fit in with the rest of the ducklings. Cast out from the family, this unhappy bird tried to find a place of acceptance and belonging, but ended up spending a miserable winter alone. When spring came, a flock of swans descended on the thawing lake. The ugly duckling, now having fully grown, couldn't endure a life of solitude and hardship anymore and so decided to throw himself at the flock of swans, thinking that it was better to be killed by such beautiful birds than to live a life of ugliness and misery. He was shocked when the swans welcomed and accepted him, only to realise by looking at his reflection in the water, that he was not an ugly duckling at all, but a majestic swan. The flock takes to the air and he spreads his magnificent wings and takes flight with the rest of his new family.

The moral of the tale: don't spend your whole life thinking you are an ugly duckling, when you are called to be a swan!

One of the main reasons we struggle with confusion over our identity, belonging and purpose is that we get our information by looking to all the wrong sources. Sometimes we can define ourselves by looking at other people – be it through social media, advertising, or by comparing ourselves to the lives of celebrities or people around us.

Other times, we can find ourselves simply looking at or within ourselves, thinking about our past life, our present circumstances or an uncertain future. All of these invariably lead to an inaccurate view of who we are.

So where can we look? The answer is that we need to go back to our Creator God, who alone knows how and why we were made. The good news is that He has not hidden these answers from us, but has actually revealed them to us in His Word – both through Jesus Christ, His living Word, and through the Bible, His written Word.

Original, fallen and transformed life

If we go to the very beginning of the Bible, we can understand something about our *original* identity, place of belonging and purpose. Here we read the following: 'So God created man in his own image, in the image of God he created him; male and female he created them. God blessed them and said to them, "Be fruitful and increase in number; fill the earth and subdue it"' (Gen. 1:27–28). In answer to the 'Who am I?' question, God affirms that in our original identity we were made in His image – lower than God, but higher than the rest of creation – in fact, we are the crown of God's creation, called to be His image-bearers on the earth. In this same passage, God answers the 'Where do I belong?' question by highlighting that we were made to belong in community. We were not created singular, but created in plurality, male and female. Then God answers the 'What am I living for?' question, by affirming that ultimately our purpose is to be His co-rulers and stewards, governing the rest of creation for His glory.

But that's only part of the answer. In Genesis 3 something tragic happened. Human beings turned their backs on their Creator, thus forfeiting their original identity, harmonious community, and divine purpose. As a result, although there are still vestiges of the original design, we all essentially live in a *fallen* condition, no longer enjoying the glory of our original state. We were made for a great cause but can no longer fulfil it.

So where does that leave us? In desperate need of rescue and restoration! Thankfully, that's exactly what Jesus Christ came to do; not just to undo the effects of the Fall, but to give us a new and *transformed* identity, community and purpose, even greater than our original design.

In the New Testament, the Gospel writers present a stunning picture of how Jesus came to the rescue: through His life and, especially, through His death and resurrection. In the book of Acts we see how the first Christians, filled with the power of the Spirit, spread the good news of Jesus, starting in Jerusalem and ending up at Rome, the capital of the empire. One of the strategic cities that the good news came to was Ephesus on the coast of what we know today as Turkey.

The gospel in Ephesus and the letter to the Ephesians

We read about the story of how the gospel came to Ephesus in Acts 19, largely through the ministry of the apostle Paul – himself radically converted to Christ earlier in the story (Acts 9). Starting with about twelve men, the message spread first throughout this influential city and then throughout the whole of the region. Once he had established the church in Ephesus, Paul's strategy was to follow up by occasionally visiting, sending some of his fellow workers and writing letters to encourage the Christians in their new-found faith. One of those letters, known in this book simply as 'Ephesians', is found in our New Testament today. It seems likely that this letter may have been a circular, sent to Christians in the whole region of Asia Minor, of which Ephesus was the centre. Contained within this short letter are some of the most comprehensive and marvellous descriptions of what it means to be transformed in and through a relationship with Jesus Christ.

The letter has a clear structure. Chapters 1–3 focus primarily on what God has done for us in Christ, chapters 4–6 on how we are to live in the light of this. We could summarise this as *transformed life* (1–3) and *transformed living* (4–6). In this book we are going to focus on Ephesians 1–3 and on the transformed life.

Ephesians 1–3 paints a wonderfully full portrait of our new identity, belonging and purpose in Christ. Many commentators have recognised the centrality of the *identity* theme in Ephesians.[1] But Paul doesn't stop with just looking at our individual transformation; rather, he proceeds to talk about God's great purposes for His people, which involves them being restored not just to Himself, but to one another, in a glorious new eternal community called Church. The great hope of Ephesians is that all those who are 'in Christ', both Jews and Gentiles (which means non-Jews), now have the privilege of *belonging* to this new family.[2] From this foundation of us knowing our new identity in Christ, and our new sense of belonging in His new community, Paul moves us to talking about our new *purpose* in Christ: a purpose that starts now, and will be fulfilled in eternity.

How to get maximum benefit from this devotional guide

The purpose of this devotional guide is to help us digest these wonderful truths in bite-sized chunks. So, every day for the next fifty days, we are going to be studying a verse or verses from Ephesians 1–3, which will help paint a picture of the transformed life. In order to benefit the most, it is important to invest the appropriate time. As well as setting aside a few minutes every day in reading each section, it is so important to follow this up by personal reflection and response. A recent survey of how people grow in their spiritual journey with Christ highlighted that the number one spiritual growth tool (twice as influential as any other practice) was the discipline of regularly reading and reflecting on Scripture.[3] If you are already in this discipline then hopefully this study will give you some extra material to use alongside your daily devotions. For others, my hope and prayer is that this will set you on a course of daily reading and reflecting on Scripture that will last a lifetime!

To get started, may I encourage you to set aside time this week to read through the whole letter to the Ephesians in one sitting. Get yourself a drink and a Bible and find somewhere quiet, then slowly read all six chapters out loud. We are using the New International Version (the Anglicised 2011 and 1984 editions) for this study, so it might help if you do the same. This will give you a great introduction to the letter and foundation for this study.

Each daily study in this devotional is concluded with Reflect and Respond points and a Memory Verse. These are designed to help us apply what we have learned to our own lives and to know Scripture by heart, more and more. At the end of each week are Action Steps and a Reflection and Prayer section. These will help us to consolidate and take further what we have personally discovered throughout the week.

In addition to this personal devotional, we have produced the following free online materials for churches and small groups to use together:

- Small group videos and study guide
- Sermon outlines
- Resources for youth

There are also activity books available for early years children (three-to six-year-olds) and primary years children (seven-to eleven-year-olds), which are written to help children understand the words of Paul in Ephesians through Bible stories and activities.

As you go through this study, my prayer for you is simply based on Paul's prayer for the Ephesians: 'I keep asking that the God of our Lord Jesus Christ, the glorious Father, may give you the Spirit of wisdom and revelation, so that you may know him better. I pray also that the eyes of your heart may be enlightened in order that you may know the hope to which he has called you, the riches of his glorious inheritance in the saints, and his incomparably great power for us who believe' (Eph. 1:17–19, NIV 1984).

BRAND NEW

'Paul, an apostle of Christ Jesus by the will of God,
To the saints in Ephesus, the faithful in Christ Jesus: Grace and
peace to you from God our Father and the Lord Jesus Christ.'

EPHESIANS 1:1–2 (NIV 1984)

A NEW PERSON

'Paul, an apostle of Christ Jesus by the will of God,
To the saints in Ephesus, the faithful in Christ Jesus:
Grace and peace to you from God our Father and
the Lord Jesus Christ.' **EPHESIANS 1:1–2 (NIV 1984)**

Transformation. A thorough, radical, dramatic change – not just a small tweak or subtle difference. To be transformed is to never be the same again.

One of my favourite pictures of transformation is that of a caterpillar to a butterfly. There's an element of continuity: it's still an insect and has the same basic DNA, but in every other respect the transformation is spectacular. As a caterpillar it was highly limited as it crawled around, eating leaves, and looking fairly drab. Now transformed into a butterfly it is free to fly around, sip nectar and look stunning! In a similar, but even more wonderful way, God has come to transform our lives, in and through Jesus Christ.

In Ephesians 1–3, the transformed life in Christ is presented to us in all its beauty. Here, in the introduction in Ephesians 1:1–2, like an overture to a symphony, Paul lays out many of the wonderful transformation themes that feature so prominently in the rest of the letter.

First, he presents himself as an example of one of the greatest transformations in history. No longer the Jewish fanatic Saul of Tarsus, who persecuted the Church even to the point of seeking out and imprisoning Christians (see Acts 8:3; 9:1–2), he is now 'Paul, an apostle of Christ Jesus by the will of God', committed to telling the good news of Jesus to a primarily Gentile audience. What a transformation!

Second, he highlights the wonderful change that has taken place in his readers. Most of them would have been Gentiles, living in and around the city of Ephesus, who had encountered Christ through Paul's ministry. Now they were no longer pagans, excluded from the privileges of the people of God, but they were 'saints … faithful in Christ Jesus.'

Third, he emphasises the glorious new relationship he and they have entered into with God Himself, characterised by these wonderful words: 'Grace and peace to you from God our Father and the Lord Jesus Christ.'

Throughout history, billions of people have experienced a transformed life through Jesus Christ. For me, although I was brought up in a Christian home, I grew up without knowing Christ personally. As a result, although I had a happy childhood, during my early teens I became aware of a deep emptiness and went through a full-scale teenage rebellion. In spite of this, I managed to do well enough at school to end up in a great university. Surrounded by privilege, prospects and people who had everything going for them, I was still aware of a deep unease and a lack of ultimate purpose. That was until I encountered Christ. In place of the inner turmoil and emptiness, my life was filled with tremendous love, joy and peace, and infused with incredible hope and meaning. In short, my life was, and still is, being completely *transformed*!

For others, their start in life was less positive and their transformation even more dramatic. Take Darrell Tunningley, for example, a former drug dealer, addict and convicted armed robber. While serving five and a half years in prison, Darrell attended an Alpha Course in HMP Wolds, where God broke into his life and changed him forever. In his book *Unreachable*, Darrell writes, 'If you have read this book because you feel that your life is going down the toilet then just stop, dare to dream what God may have in store for you. Remember a heroin addict who was convicted for armed robbery, God came into his life, gave him a future that he would never have dreamt of.'[4] Darrell is a wonderful example of a life that has been transformed by Christ.

Your story will be different from mine and Darrell's. Your need of transformation may be more or less obvious, and your conversion experience may be a lot more, or less, dramatic. But the good news is that wherever you are on your spiritual journey, your life can be transformed.

REFLECT AND RESPOND

- **If you have experienced the transformation that comes from encountering Christ, thank God for how He has already worked in your life. Pray that, over the next fifty days of these studies, He would continue to move in your life.**

- **If you have not personally encountered God, but would like to, you can start with this simple prayer: 'God, please show me who You are, so that I may know You. Amen.'**

MEMORY VERSE

'To the saints in Ephesus, the faithful in Christ Jesus: Grace and peace to you from God our Father and the Lord Jesus Christ.'
EPHESIANS 1:1–2 (NIV 1984)

A NEW IDENTITY

'To the saints in Ephesus, the faithful in Christ Jesus'
EPHESIANS 1:1 (NIV 1984)

Many people want to know their true identity. One of the BBC's most successful and long-running documentaries is entitled *Who Do You Think You Are?* In this programme, celebrities are encouraged to discover something of their identity by looking back at their family history. However, while entertaining to viewers and enlightening to those involved, it provides a very limited answer to this all-important question of how we can discover our true identity.

A more helpful, accurate and comprehensive answer is provided by the apostle Paul. Inspired by the Holy Spirit, he starts his letter to the Ephesians by showing that this issue of identity is central to his concern. But unlike the BBC programme, he doesn't point us to our family tree. Unlike modern-day advertising or social media, he doesn't tell us to compare ourselves with others. Unlike modern-day self-help gurus or psychologists, he doesn't tell us to 'look within ourselves'. Instead, writing to Christians, he highlights the centrality of knowing what it means to be 'in Christ Jesus'.

It has been estimated that when all of Paul's writings are examined, the phrase 'in Christ' and its variations (such as 'in him', 'in whom', 'in the Beloved') occur 216 times; whereas he refers to 'Christians' only three times. In the letter to the Ephesians alone, Paul spoke of believers as being 'in Christ' twelve times overtly and twenty-two other times in various forms.

So it is clear that this phrase holds huge significance. And the biggest difference from all of those other methods of seeking our *true* identity, is that Jesus' way involves being given a *new* identity. You could say, it's not who you are but *whose* you are. Being 'in Christ', that is unified with Him, we become *who He says we are.* And what He says is what we are going to find out over the next few weeks!

Throughout Ephesians 1–3, Paul paints a marvellous portrait of our new identity in Christ (see the Summary in Day 50). In the NIV 1984 translation of today's verse, Paul starts by declaring that those in Christ are now 'saints'. This at first may seem very strange. After all, we normally think of saints as very special people, a rare breed, who posthumously receive the designation 'Saint'. Yet remarkably Paul is saying that anyone who has become a Christian is actually a saint, which means that they are now sanctified (made clean) and set apart for God.

This is different to the way that many Christians view themselves. Rather than seeing themselves as 'saints … in Christ', it is popular to refer to oneself as a 'sinner saved by grace' or simply as a sinner. We can sympathise to a degree with this description. After all, we should be keen to stress that our becoming a Christian was an act of God's grace alone and not something that was merited. Nevertheless, Paul does not address this letter to the 'sinners saved by grace' but to the 'saints'.

Why does this matter? Because if you see yourself as a sinner saved by grace, you are more likely to live as a struggling sinner. But if you see yourself as a sinner who through grace has not only been saved but in Christ has been made new, you will start to live in the light of your new identity. This is crucial to understanding Paul's whole approach here in Ephesians and indeed elsewhere in his letters. He doesn't start by focusing on our need for behavioural change, but rather on our change of identity. Hence, throughout the whole of chapters 1–3 he is primarily concerned with the transformation that has already taken place through Christ. Then, and only then, does he begin in chapters 4–6 to focus on a transformed lifestyle. His method is clear. First, know who God says you are – a saint and a new person – then, live like one.

REFLECT AND RESPOND

- **How do you think that knowing you are 'in Christ' will begin to change your answer to 'Who am I?'**

- **Now that you know you are a 'saint' how do you think you might start living differently?**

MEMORY VERSE

'To the saints in Ephesus, the faithful in Christ Jesus: Grace and peace to you from God our Father and the Lord Jesus Christ.'
EPHESIANS 1:1–2 (NIV 1984)

A NEW PURPOSE

'To the saints in Ephesus, the faithful in Christ Jesus'
EPHESIANS 1:1 (NIV 1984)

William Wilberforce, Martin Luther King and Mother Teresa all had this in common: they not only found and fulfilled their unique life purpose, but each of them discovered the universal purpose for life, summarised here by Paul as being 'faithful in Christ Jesus'.

Finding and fulfilling one's life purpose is not just something reserved for a special few. Yet tragically, many live and die never having discovered, let alone having lived out, their life purpose. Some struggle with a lack of purpose, with sometimes devastating consequences. In August 2011, riots broke out in London and then spread right across England. While there were many contributing factors, one journalist highlighted the fact that some rioters simply 'had nothing else to do with themselves'. This may be an example of a more extreme consequence, but a lack of purpose is prevalent today, and is a cause of much unhappiness. It explains, in part, why we can have so much entertainment available to us, but can still be so bored; why we can have so much choice, but still find little that seems to satisfy.

If a lack of purpose is a major problem, then so too is a misplaced sense of purpose. Much of our culture today is dominated by living *for* oneself in the total pursuit of personal fulfilment and success. But we were called, like William Wilberforce, Martin Luther King and Mother Teresa, to live lives of great significance, living *beyond* ourselves in the service of God and others.

As with the question of identity (Day 2), Paul makes it clear that our true and transformed purpose can only be found by us being 'in Christ'. In the words of Ephesians 1:11, 'It's in Christ that we find out who we are and what we are living for' (*The Message*). This theme of purpose is something that Paul highlights throughout Ephesians 1–3. In 1:9–10, he talks about God's eternal purpose, in 2:10, he refers to our eternal purpose, and in 3:1–13 he introduces the concept that we each have a specific life purpose. Here, in this overture in Ephesians 1:1, Paul simply highlights that at the heart of life's purpose is the need to be 'faithful' in Christ. This word 'faithful', like the word 'faith', is linked to the concept of having trust or of being trustworthy. Put simply, to be faithful in Christ Jesus – to trust and be trustworthy – is to live a life of ultimate purpose.

First, to be faithful involves putting our faith or trust in Christ. Some mistakenly think of faith as simply intellectual assent to certain propositions. However, while New Testament faith does include an agreement with certain doctrines about Christ, it goes beyond this to include a full reliance upon Christ's person and redemptive work. Let me illustrate. Every time you sit down in a chair you are exercising faith, by placing your full confidence in the fact that the chair will hold you up. It's not enough just to know, conceptually, that the chair will sustain you. Rather, you have to put your faith or trust in practice by actually sitting down! In the same way, when someone becomes a Christian they are making an active decision to trust in the faithfulness of Christ to uphold them and transform them in every area of their lives – past, present and future. I remember when I first became a Christian, I prayed a prayer that was in effect a prayer of trust – 'Lord, I trust You more than I trust myself to run my life from now on.'

But there is a second aspect of the term 'faithful in Christ' and it can mean that Christians are faithful in the sense that they will keep the faith, and stay true or loyal to Christ and His purpose for their lives. This can be a concern for some people. They think they can't become a Christian because they can't keep it up! But this is why we need to make sure that we understand that Christianity is not about us trying harder, but more trusting in Christ to keep us trustworthy. In effect, it highlights the *transformation* that takes place when someone becomes a Christian, and that we don't just have *our* resources but the resources of His Holy Spirit to help us stay faithful.

REFLECT AND RESPOND

- **Take time to consider what it means to be 'faithful' in Christ.**

- **Have you trusted and are you trusting in Jesus right now?**

- **Are you loyal to Christ in your daily life? Ask for the Spirit's help to grow in this.**

MEMORY VERSE

'To the saints in Ephesus, the faithful in Christ Jesus: Grace and peace to you from God our Father and the Lord Jesus Christ.'
EPHESIANS 1:1–2 (NIV 1984)

BELONGING TO A NEW FAMILY

'To the saints in Ephesus, the faithful in Christ Jesus: Grace and peace to you from God our Father and the Lord Jesus Christ.' **EPHESIANS 1:1–2 (NIV 1984)**

On Day 2 we started to answer the 'Who am I?' or *identity* question and on Day 3 we looked at the 'What am I living for?' or *purpose* question. Today, we will begin to explore the 'Where do I belong?' or *belonging* question. One of our basic needs as human beings is the longing to belong. This goes right back to God's original plan for creation, where God created mankind as male and female to live in community together. Put simply, we were formed for family, we were created for community and we were made to belong.

So why then is there so much isolation, loneliness and relational disharmony? There is much that can be said about this, but the root of the problem goes back to what is called the 'Fall' of humankind (see the Introduction). This resulted not only in a broken relationship with God, but also brought strife and dislocation to human relationships. This has been a problem throughout the ages, but the situation is often made much worse in modern Western society. Unlike in many Eastern cultures where the extended family is still very strong, in the West there has been a narrowing down to the so-called 'nuclear family'. More recently, with fewer people getting married and more people getting divorced, the cohesion and security of the nuclear family itself has been under threat.

Into this situation of relational strife, family breakdown, and isolation, Paul's picture of the transformed life comes to us as a blessed relief. In addition to us enjoying a new identity and purpose in Christ, we now have the privilege of belonging to a new family. This communal perspective is so inherent in this letter that it is easy for those of us with a Western mindset to skip over words like 'saints' (plural!) and phrases like 'God *our* Father' and miss the obvious: Paul is not writing to individual Christians but to the *Christian community*!

Of course, this doesn't mean that there aren't vital lessons for us as individuals, but we must understand this teaching in the light of our belonging to the community of God's people. When Paul talks about the saints, he is writing with a Jewish understanding of the 'people of God', but is saying to primarily Gentile believers: 'you now belong to the called out, holy, people of God.' When he refers to God as 'our Father', Paul is similarly highlighting that all Christians, himself included, are part of the 'family of God' of which God is the Father.

This is of huge significance and goes right to the heart of our need to belong, in particular, to belong to the Church. The Church is not – as it has sometimes been portrayed – a religious organisation or a building. No! The Church is the people of God – the family of God. Once you become a Christian, you are born again into and belong to this *universal*, eternal family. But in order to actually enjoy the benefits of belonging, you need to be actively part of a *local* church (see Day 13 and Week 5 for more on this). This means that Church is not simply a weekly meeting to turn up to when you feel like it, but is a family in which you are actively to give and receive. That is one of the reasons why this study comes with free online small group resources and focuses on learning in small groups. It's not just that we will learn better when we are learning with others but it is in a small group setting that we can start rediscovering something of how God designed family, and extended family, as the best context in which to do life.

There are many aspects to this. But for now let me encourage you to view your group not just as a meeting to attend or a place to receive content, but somewhere you can start experiencing real community –

where you can share joys and hardship, where you can pray, worship, eat and witness together.

Moreover, when you do come to the wider gathering of the Church family at weekend services, take time to appreciate the wonder of the fact that this is a representation of a worldwide, eternal family to which you now *belong*!

REFLECT AND RESPOND

- **If you are in a small group, how could you show your appreciation for the leaders and members this week?**

- **Do you know anyone who has stopped coming to church? How could you encourage them to start again?**

- **Pray for your church to be a place of belonging.**

MEMORY VERSE

'To the saints in Ephesus, the faithful in Christ Jesus: Grace and peace to you from God our Father and the Lord Jesus Christ.'
EPHESIANS 1:1–2 (NIV 1984)

DAY 5

LIVING IN THE GRACE OF GOD

'Grace and peace to you from God our Father and the Lord Jesus Christ.' **EPHESIANS 1:2**

It has been reported that many years ago, during a British conference on comparative religions, experts from around the world were discussing whether any one belief was unique to the Christian faith. They began eliminating possibilities. Incarnation? Other religions had different versions of gods appearing in human form. Resurrection? Again, other religions had accounts of return from death. The debate went on for some time, until C.S. Lewis wandered into the room. 'What's the rumpus about?' he asked, and heard in reply that his colleagues were discussing Christianity's unique contribution among world religions. In his forthright manner, Lewis responded, 'Oh, that's easy. It's grace.'[5]

So, what is grace? At its heart, grace is the undeserved favour of God. It was a concept that was at the heart of Paul's own experience and was central to his whole teaching. Paul knew that he had become a Christian on the road to Damascus, not because he earned it, but because of the unmerited favour of God. So, when he greets his readers with 'Grace … to you', he is not simply saying something nice at the start of his letter, he is revealing from first to last that the Christian life is based on the grace that comes from God our Father and the Lord Jesus Christ.

This undeserved favour works on a number of levels. First, grace is the key to how we are saved. Contrary to how we often think, and to what religion tends to teach, our salvation is not something that we deserve or earn; rather, it is through grace. This is so central that throughout the early part of his letter, Paul emphasises this again and again. Note the following verses:

- 'to the praise of his glorious grace, which he has freely given us in the One he loves' (1:6)
- 'in accordance with the riches of God's grace that he lavished on us' (1:7–8)
- 'it is by grace you have been saved' (2:5)
- 'the incomparable riches of his grace' (2:7)
- 'For it is by grace you have been saved, through faith' (2:8)

Paul is so overwhelmed by saving grace that he not only repeatedly refers to it, but he piles on the superlatives: 'glorious grace', 'the riches of God's grace', 'the incomparable riches of his grace.'

But the great news is that grace is not just the means by which we are saved and become Christians. Here in Ephesians 1:2 Paul is writing to those who were already saved by grace, yet he still blesses them with 'Grace … *from* God the Father and our Lord Jesus Christ' (emphasis added). This highlights that we don't just need the unmerited favour of God to start the journey, but the *ongoing* favour of God to empower us as we continue on the journey. Put simply, we need His favour and enabling power to live out the transformed life. Significantly, like two bookends, Paul begins this letter with 'Grace … to you' (1:2) and ends with 'Grace to all who love our Lord Jesus Christ with an undying love' (6:24). Why? Because from first to last the Christian life is all about grace.

I am personally very aware of the ongoing grace of God in my life. Not only am I so conscious and grateful that I have been saved by grace, but on an almost daily basis I am overwhelmed by the fact that I am being sustained by grace. Whatever may have happened the day before, or whatever the challenges of tomorrow, I know that I can approach each day confident in the knowledge that I am a highly favoured child of God and my life is being empowered and protected by His ongoing, amazing grace. I am also very conscious that I am not just saved by grace and sustained by grace, but I am also specifically called by grace. Paul highlights this idea of grace for our life calling or ministry in chapter 3:

- 'Surely you have heard about the administration of God's grace that was given to me for you' (3:2)
- 'I became a servant of this gospel by the gift of God's grace' (3:7)

In summary, we are saved by grace, sustained by grace and called by grace.

REFLECT AND RESPOND

- **Take some time today to reflect upon and rejoice in the grace of God.**

- **Are there any specific situations you are currently facing in which you need more grace, or particular people you need to show more grace towards? Ask God for His help in these areas.**

MEMORY VERSE

'To the saints in Ephesus, the faithful in Christ Jesus: Grace and peace to you from God our Father and the Lord Jesus Christ.'
EPHESIANS 1:1–2 (NIV 1984)

ENJOYING THE PEACE OF GOD

'Grace and peace to you from God our Father and the Lord Jesus Christ.' **EPHESIANS 1:2**

Peace is something that we all desperately need and long for. For those of us born after 1945, it is easy to take for granted that we have not lived through the suffering of the world wars that previous generations suffered. For those of us living in the West, we can also too readily forget that many troubled regions of the world are still torn apart by war.

Yet, as important as this absence of war is, the peace that is available to us through Christ is much deeper and broader. When Paul introduces his letter by blessing his readers with grace and 'peace' he is using the Greek word *eirene*, which is similar in meaning to the Hebrew word *shalom*. Biblical shalom is about far more than the cessation of conflict or even an inner feeling of tranquillity. Rather, it carries with it the idea of wholeness, wellbeing and the idea that life can be lived as God intended it. We can define this peace as operating in three dimensions: eternally, internally and externally!

The first dimension of 3D shalom is *eternal peace*, or peace with God. This is foundational. The Bible presents a picture of how, because of mankind's rebellion against the Creator, we have all fallen short of His standards and are under His judgment (see Rom. 3:23; Heb. 9:27). That is fundamentally why Christ came to die in our place and bring peace and reconciliation between us and God. In the words of Romans 5:1, Paul says that 'since we have been justified through faith, we have peace with God through our Lord Jesus Christ'. Because Jesus was raised from the dead, we know that the price for our sins was paid in full on the cross. Therefore, in Christ we are no longer at enmity with God, but are eternally at peace with Him.

Once we know this eternal peace with God, only then can we know true *internal peace*, or peace with ourselves. This inner peace is of course something we all desire, but sadly it often proves elusive. There is an extraordinary restlessness within human beings, which makes us unable to experience peace. The great French thinker Pascal said this: 'All of humanity's problems stem from man's inability to sit quietly in a room alone.'[6] Our lack of peace drives us to greed, selfishness, materialism, sexual immorality, foolish ambition and so on. We search for peace in all the wrong places. One of the most highly acclaimed pop songs is U2's 1987 track *I Still Haven't Found What I'm Looking For*. Its popularity, it seems, is not just because of the music but because it somehow echoes a cry in our culture today.

The good news is that Jesus comes to satisfy that cry, giving us a deep sense of inner peace and fulfilment. This peace is a peace that is independent of circumstances. The world's peace can only be produced by externals such as prosperity and tranquillity; God's peace can be felt in the heat of the battle and on the way to the operating theatre. When we choose not to worry but to turn to Him in prayer, we can enjoy 'the peace of God, which transcends all understanding' (Phil. 4:7).

Then, when we are enjoying eternal and internal peace, we can start manifesting an *external peace*, a peace in our relationships with others. This relational peace is central to Paul's message in Ephesians, particularly in 2:11–22, where he depicts Christ as 'our peace', bringing down the barrier between Jews and Gentiles and uniting them together in Him. Similarly, today, Christ's peace is available to bring the end of racism and racial conflict, and unite all people under God. Closer to home, when we know God's peace in our own lives, we can be agents of peace and reconciliation with those around us.

Moreover, we can be those who carry the 'gospel of peace' (Eph. 6:15) into a lost and fractured world.

All of this – eternal, internal and external peace – and more, is wrapped up in this marvellous greeting: 'grace and peace to you from God our Father and the Lord Jesus Christ.'

REFLECT AND RESPOND

- **Think about this wonderful peace that Christ has come to bring.**

- **In which dimension or area do you particularly need more peace: eternal, internal or external, or all three?**

MEMORY VERSE

'To the saints in Ephesus, the faithful in Christ Jesus: Grace and peace to you from God our Father and the Lord Jesus Christ.'
EPHESIANS 1:1–2 (NIV 1984)

TRANSFORMED
BY ANOTHER

'Paul, an apostle of Christ Jesus by the will of God,
To the saints in Ephesus, the faithful in Christ Jesus:
Grace and peace to you from God our Father and
the Lord Jesus Christ.' **EPHESIANS 1:1–2 (NIV 1984)**

As we come to the close of Week 1, I want to ask you a critical question: who or what is at the centre of your life, your world, your 'universe'? For nearly 2,000 years, Western thinking was dominated by the mistaken belief in an earth-centred universe. That was until, in the sixteenth century, a new idea was proposed by the Polish astronomer Nicolaus Copernicus (1473–1543) that the sun, not the earth, was at the centre of the solar system. We may laugh at the astronomical ignorance of previous generations, but sadly, much of our culture today is dominated by a more serious misapprehension: that we as human beings are at the centre of our world, and that the most important thing in our lives is what suits us, and that everyone and everything has to revolve around us. It can therefore be quite a shock when we start reading Ephesians – especially when we come to know the God of Ephesians – to realise that He is at the centre and not us.

Allowing God to take His rightful place at the centre of our lives is key to understanding and enjoying a transformed life. A hurried reading of Ephesians and of this introduction in 1:1–2 can cause us to miss this obvious and crucial point: that the focus and the hero is not Paul, and it's certainly not the Christians, but it is the God who has revealed Himself in and through Jesus Christ. Just in these first two verses, God is referred to twice, first simply as 'God' and then as 'God our Father'. 'Christ Jesus' is mentioned three times, highlighting for Paul the wondrous truth that the long-awaited Messiah is none other than Jesus of Nazareth. The third reference includes the fuller designation, the 'Lord' Jesus Christ, indicating that He was not just a human Messiah, but that He was and is God.

Why was Paul so magnificently obsessed with Christ? Because it was through an encounter with the risen and ascended Jesus on the road to Damascus that his life had been totally transformed (Acts 9:5). Before this, he mistakenly thought that in persecuting Christ's followers, he was doing God's will. After this, he realised that Christ was the key to knowing God and enjoying the transformed life.

This move from a self-centred world-view to a Christ-centred one, is also critical for us, too, if we are to know God and enjoy the transformed life. For me, personally, knowing that I was not at the centre of my world actually came as a huge relief. Before I became a Christian, the number one thing I needed saving from was selfishness. I was my greatest problem! When I came to Christ, it was so liberating to know that I didn't have to live with me at the centre. It was such a blessing to know that from then on, I didn't have to live my life with my will and my agenda as the driving force of my life.

Over the years, I have cultivated a deeper awareness of Christ at the centre. One of the key ways has been to develop a daily appreciation of who He is and what He has done for me. I try to start each day with time listening to Him through His Word, the Bible, and speaking to Him in worship and prayer. I regularly turn to Him throughout my day, thanking Him for what He has already done in me, and asking for His help in growing to be more like Him, and in fulfilling His purpose for my life. In short, I – like Paul, the Ephesians, and the many before and since – have been and am being 'transformed by another'.

REFLECT AND RESPOND

- **If you are still at the centre of your world, then take time today to surrender fully to Christ. Whether you've done so before or not, why not invite Jesus, right now, to take centre stage in your life?**

- **In prayer, hold out your hands in front of you and give control of your life over to Him.**

MEMORY VERSE

'To the saints in Ephesus, the faithful in Christ Jesus: Grace and peace to you from God our Father and the Lord Jesus Christ.'
EPHESIANS 1:1–2 (NIV 1984)

WEEK 1 ACTION STEPS

1. If you want to become a Christian, you can. Follow this prayer, focused around three key words: admit, believe, commit. You can pray this on your own, or you can ask another Christian to pray with you: 'Lord Jesus, I admit my need of You and invite You to come and forgive me today. I believe that You died and rose again so that I could receive new peace, hope, joy and purpose. Please come into my life today. I commit to follow You all the days of my life. Amen!'

2. Take time to reflect upon the three foundational questions: 'Who am I?', 'Where do I belong?' and 'What am I living for?' (see the Introduction for more on these). Mark yourself on a scale of 1–10 as to where you think you are right now.

Concerning the **identity** question: 'Who am I?'
I feel …

(1) ——————————— (5) ——————————— (10)

| VERY INSECURE | NOT VERY SECURE | FAIRLY SECURE | VERY SECURE |

Concerning the **belonging** question: 'Where do I belong?'
I feel …

(1) ——————————— (5) ——————————— (10)

| VERY UNSURE | NOT VERY SURE | FAIRLY SURE | VERY SURE |

Concerning the **purpose** question: 'What am I living for?'
I feel …

(1) ——————————— (5) ——————————— (10)

| VERY UNSURE | NOT VERY SURE | FAIRLY SURE | VERY SURE |

REFLECTION

Jot down anything that particularly spoke to you this week and anything you have discovered about your identity, belonging and purpose.

PRAYER

Is there anything you would like to thank God for or ask Him for? If you want, write your prayer down here. This can be a good way of being able to look back and see what God has done.

WEEK 2

ETERNALLY
BLESSED

'Praise be to the God and Father of our Lord Jesus Christ, who has blessed us in the heavenly realms with every spiritual blessing in Christ. For he chose us in him before the creation of the world to be holy and blameless in his sight. In love he predestined us to for adoption to sonship through Jesus Christ, in accordance with his pleasure and will – to the praise of his glorious grace, which he has freely given us in the One he loves. In him we have redemption through his blood, the forgiveness of sins, in accordance with the riches of God's grace that he lavished on us. With all wisdom and understanding, he made known to us the mystery of his will according to his good pleasure, which he purposed in Christ, to be put into effect when the times reach their fulfilment – to bring unity all things in heaven and on earth under Christ. In him we were also chosen, having been predestined according to the plan of him who works out everything in conformity with the purpose of his will, in order that we, who were the first to put our hope in Christ, might be for the praise of his glory. And you also were included in Christ when you heard the message of truth, the gospel of your salvation. When you believed, you were marked in him with a seal, the promised Holy Spirit, who is a deposit guaranteeing our inheritance until the redemption of those who are God's possession – to the praise of his glory.'

EPHESIANS 1:3–14

DAY 8

AMAZINGLY BLESSED

'Praise be to the God and Father of our Lord Jesus Christ, who has blessed us in the heavenly realms with every spiritual blessing in Christ.' **EPHESIANS 1:3**

A few years ago some friends of ours were treated to an all expenses paid week on the luxury island of Necker in the Caribbean, personally hosted by Richard Branson. From the private jet through to the stunning accommodation, to the sumptuous food and the glorious setting, they were very happy and grateful recipients of a week of tremendous blessings. Sounds amazing, doesn't it? Our study this week highlights that we have been *far more blessed* than that! Our blessings were planned before the beginning of time, were paid for in history by Jesus, and are promised to last for eternity, and they far outweigh even a week on a luxury Caribbean island!

This may surprise you, especially if you have grown up with a view of Christianity as essentially something rather repressive or dull. Or it may be that, like Paul's hearers in Ephesus and the surrounding region, you have grown up in a religious system or with a spiritual world-view, where 'God' or the 'gods' need pleasing and can be persuaded or manipulated by certain spiritual activities or religious acts. If so, the good news is that this is *not* the God of the Bible.

Right from Genesis 1, we see God as a good Creator who wants to bless humanity. Here in Ephesians 1, God's desire to bless those who are now part of His new creation in Christ is stunningly confirmed.

This would have been a huge relief to the first-century Ephesians and is a huge relief to us in the twenty-first century, too.

With this as a backdrop it is significant that Paul starts the main part of this letter (after the introduction), with what is essentially one long, long sentence of blessing. It's as if the apostle is so full of what God has done for us that he barely pauses for breath! Notice that all three Persons of the Trinity are involved in us being blessed. First, it is God the Father who is the source or origin of all the blessings. Second, it is the Lord Jesus Christ, our Saviour, who is the one through whom all these blessings are mediated to us. Third, these blessings come through the Holy Spirit, since these blessings are spiritual, meaning Spirit-given. Significant, too, is the fact that these blessings are mentioned as being in the heavenly realms. This is a term unique to Paul's letter to the Ephesians and is mentioned five times (1:3,20; 2:6; 3:10; 6:12). It is widely recognised that this emphasis is written here because of the magical and occult background that many of these largely Gentile Christians would have been saved from. Here, Paul is reassuring the believers that they are blessed by God, in Christ, through the Spirit in the heavenly realms – that is, in the very sphere where they were previously controlled by spiritual forces of evil (see 2:2; 6:12). Now in Christ, they are blessed and victorious.

Finally, it is crucial to note the tense that this is written in. The blessings are not primarily for the future, although they include future blessings as we shall see in Day 14, but they are blessings that have been given in the past and therefore can be enjoyed in the present – in other words, right now. This is great news. It means that we don't have to twist God's arm to bless us, since we are already blessed! It doesn't mean that we are necessarily experiencing all these blessings right now, but they are now available for us to enjoy.

It is so important that we begin to grasp how good God is, and, like Paul, to live lives full of praise and gratitude for His goodness and blessings towards us. In life, where there are still so many challenges, it is easy to look at our circumstances and feel disappointed or aggrieved. It is tempting to look at others and feel jealous of how blessed they seem, and hope that we too might be given a free week on Necker Island or the like! But the reality is that we have already been blessed *beyond measure*!

REFLECT AND RESPOND

- **Develop an attitude of gratitude. Why not start by thanking God for how much He has already blessed you in Christ?**

- **What practical steps could you take to get into the daily habit of thanking God for all His gifts and blessings? (Putting reminders on your phone or sticky notes, for example.)**

MEMORY VERSE

'Praise be to the God and Father of our Lord Jesus Christ, who has blessed us in the heavenly realms with every spiritual blessing in Christ.'

EPHESIANS 1:3

CHOSEN TO BE HOLY

'For he chose us in him before the creation of the world to be holy and blameless in his sight. In love he predestined us to be adopted as his sons'
EPHESIANS 1:4–5 (NIV 1984)

There's a clip in a German comedy show of an elderly gentleman in a kitchen, who, much to the horror of his daughter, proceeds to use an iPad as a chopping board, before putting it in the dishwasher to be cleaned! I don't know whether you have received an item and you didn't know what it was for. That is, until you read the maker's instructions. It's the same for our lives. If we really want to understand our true identity, place of belonging and life purpose, we have to go back and read carefully our Maker's instructions.

Ephesians 1:3–14 is one of the best places to discover God's plan for our lives. Here in Ephesians 1:4–5, we see God *chose us to be holy*. In fact, before we ever chose God, He had a purpose for our lives and chose us to be holy and blameless in Christ 'before the creation of the world'. What a staggering and comforting thought! This has some massive implications.

First, it means that you are not an accident and you are not unwanted. Your parents may not have planned for you, but God chose you before He made the world. People may have spurned you, but God wanted you to be 'in Christ'. Knowing this is a key to enjoying a greater sense of identity and security.

But second, notice that His purpose in choosing us in Christ was so that we would 'be holy and blameless in his sight'. Bear in mind that none of us were born holy and blameless! Hence, if we are to live up to God's great design for us, we must be *transformed*. This is what happens when we accept Christ. We immediately become saints, set apart for Him. But this initial holiness is clearly meant to lead to a lifetime of progressive and practical holiness, resulting in full and final holiness when Christ returns.

Knowing that we have been made holy (set apart), are being made holy (in our character and lifestyle) and will be finally made holy (perfected) has huge implications for how we are to live. It means that we should never see ourselves primarily as sinners but rather as saints (see Day 2). It means that while we are not going to arrive at total or sinless perfection in this life, we now have a new identity and a new power to overcome sin. This doesn't mean that we will grow in holiness without any effort on our part, but rather have a choice to live the new life that God has given us (see Eph. 4:22–24). If this is why the Father chose us, then let's live up to this high calling. Let's pray, read the Bible, listen to the Spirit, obey His promptings and live the new life.

So, what does this life of holiness look like? A key is found in the next phrase 'in love'. In the NIV, this is linked to the next verse, 'in love he predestined us', implying that it is talking about *God's* love for us. Other translations and many commentators link the 'in love' to the previous phrase, ('holy and blameless before him in love' in the NRSV) indicating that this is talking about *our* love. Both meanings are true, but if this verse is referring to 'our love' it is hugely helpful for us in understanding what a transformed life will look like. It is not a life that is dominated by rules and regulations, but rather a Spirit-filled life that will be expressed in love – for God and for other people. This was the life that Jesus lived and commanded for us (John 13:34–35), and this was the life that the writers of the New Testament regularly commended for the believers in Christ. Later in Ephesians, Paul puts it this way: 'Follow Christ's example, therefore, as dearly loved children, and live a life of love, just as Christ loved us and gave himself up for us as a fragrant offering and sacrifice to God' (Eph. 5:1–2).

REFLECT AND RESPOND

- Today, reflect and rejoice in the fact that God has chosen you in Christ.

- Make either a new or renewed decision to live as He intended you to: a life that is increasingly holy and blameless and characterised by love.

MEMORY VERSE

'Praise be to the God and Father of our Lord Jesus Christ, who has blessed us in the heavenly realms with every spiritual blessing in Christ.'

EPHESIANS 1:3

DAY 10

ADOPTED

'For he chose us in him before the creation of the world to be holy and blameless in his sight. In love he predestined us for adoption to sonship through Jesus Christ, in accordance with his pleasure and will – to the praise of his glorious grace, which he has freely given us in the One he loves.' **EPHESIANS 1:4–6**

One of the most exciting days of my life was when I was nine years old. My mum and dad came back with a 'present' – a new, adopted baby brother. This nine-month-old boy was immediately given a new name, had new parents, and had a new family, including a very proud older brother. He also shared in all the blessings of our family and not only enjoyed eating at our table, but seemed to delight in throwing portions of his food around the dining room!

While recognising that many struggle with relating to their earthly fathers, and acknowledging that there are challenges with natural adoption, the great news is that our spiritual adoption by God the Father is entirely positive and is one of the great blessings of the transformed life. Before we were in Christ, we were enslaved by sin, spiritually rejected, insecure and alone. Now that we are in Christ, we have a new identity as beloved children – accepted, loved and secure. We have a new Father, the perfect Dad, the best Dad in the universe, the all-loving, all-powerful Dad. We have a new older brother, Jesus Christ. We also have a new spiritual family, the Church.

44

One of the worst aspects of the Fall and of our fallen identity is a sense of spiritual rejection that goes back to mankind's expulsion from the Garden of Eden (see Gen. 3:24). This is gloriously reversed through the knowledge that in Christ, the Father planned for, or 'predestined', us to be adopted as His children.

The great missionary leader Floyd McClung used to say to his young adopted child that he had chosen him specifically, in contrast to other parents who got whom they were given! The child was so thrilled at this thought that he would boast at school about how he had been adopted and chosen.

A class of school children were discussing a picture of a family. One little boy in the picture had different colour hair from the other family members in the picture. One child suggested that he was adopted and a little girl said, 'I know all about adoptions because I was adopted.' 'What does it mean to be adopted?' asked another child. 'It means,' said the girl, 'that I grew in my mummy's heart instead of her tummy!' How profound.

The great news is that you were in God the Father's heart not only before you were born, but before the creation of the world. Listen to these amazing words in *The Message* paraphrase: 'Long before he laid down earth's foundations, he had us in mind, had settled on us as the focus of his love … Long, long ago he decided to adopt us into his family through Jesus Christ. (What pleasure he took in planning this!)' (Eph. 1:4–6). I love this picture of God's delight in planning for us to become His sons and daughters, at the same time as He chose us in Christ even before the creation of the world. What a staggering thought!

Central to the ancient Roman idea of adoption was the concept of inheritance. We will look in more detail at this on Day 19, but for now, it's important to grasp that in becoming God's children (His 'sons'), we all, male and female, now share in the inheritance of Jesus, the firstborn Son. Moreover, He paid the ultimate price for us to become His children by sending His own Son to die for us in order to rescue us. In fact, the whole plan of redemption can be summarised in this statement:

'the Son of God became the son of man, that we, the sons and daughters of men, might become the sons and daughters of God.'

In his classic work *Knowing God*, Jim Packer describes the doctrine of justification – being forgiven and righteous – as the primary or fundamental blessing of the gospel, and the doctrine of spiritual adoption, whereby we become children of God, as the highest blessing of the gospel. Packer poses the question: 'What is a Christian?' then answers 'A Christian is one who has God as Father'.[7]

REFLECT AND RESPOND

- **As you reflect today, consider these words: 'You are a wanted, chosen, planned for, dearly loved child of God.'**

- **Why not write down these words and repeat them to yourself throughout your day: 'I am a chosen, planned for, dearly loved child of God.'**

MEMORY VERSE

'Praise be to the God and Father of our Lord Jesus Christ, who has blessed us in the heavenly realms with every spiritual blessing in Christ.'

EPHESIANS 1:3

REDEEMED AND FORGIVEN

'In him we have redemption through his blood, the forgiveness of sins, in accordance with the riches of God's grace that he lavished on us.' **EPHESIANS 1:7–8**

Today, we continue to look at the amazing blessings with which God has blessed us in Christ, in particular at the blessings of redemption and forgiveness.

The concept of redemption – freedom from slavery through the payment of a price – was a widespread concept in the ancient world, where slave-owning was common. For the Jews who had been freed from slavery in Egypt by the mighty hand of God, and protected from judgment through the sprinkling of lamb's blood, it had an extra depth of meaning. However, to those with a modern-day Western mindset, such a concept is harder to grasp. So, let me tell you a story from another culture to illustrate.

Garra was a slave of the great African chief, Libe. To evade his cruel owner's anger he escaped, was pursued, captured and was being led back in chains, when an English trader offered gold for his ransom. Libe addressed the trader: 'Man of the pale face, I seek not your gold. I need blood.' At Libe's sign an archer prepared an arrow to shoot at the trembling Garra. The Englishman saw it, and thrust his arm between it and the slave and drew blood. Libe raised his hands in amazement. He knew the trader was well known, and his name esteemed in that area. Looking Libe full in the face, the trader said, 'You seek blood, there it flows. I claim your slave.' Then turning to the slave, he said, 'Garra, you have been bought by my blood, your life which belongs to me, I give to you.'[8]

When Paul says that in Christ we have 'redemption through his blood', he was saying something similar but far more wonderful. We, like the Jews in Egypt and Garra in Africa, were slaves, but to even worse tyrants: the world, the flesh and the devil (see Eph. 2:1–2). That was until Jesus Christ, the only completely righteous man who ever lived, paid the highest possible price. He died in our place, shedding His blood, not just temporarily from one part of His body, but from His back, His head, His wrists, His feet, as He hung in indescribable agony, shamefully naked on a cross. Why? To buy us back and set us free.

Central to this freedom was 'the forgiveness of sins'. Here's the reality: all of us have sinned, and the ultimate price of sin is death (Rom. 3:23; 6:23). Now that Christ has died in our place we can be and are forgiven – completely and eternally. This means that there is no sin that you and I have committed that can't be forgiven. Consider the worst thing that you have ever done: the most shameful action you have ever undertaken. If you are in Christ then He has paid the penalty, so that you don't need to. So, don't carry the guilt or the shame anymore, but instead praise God for His blessing of forgiveness.

If the emphasis here is on redemption being linked to the forgiveness of sins, it is worth noting that to be redeemed means more than being forgiven. In fact, Jesus Himself taught that He had come to free us not just from the *penalty* but also from the *power* of sin (John 8:36). In other words, whatever used to enslave us – selfishness, fear, addiction, anger – need no longer have a hold on us. We can choose to go free. What a blessing!

In case we wondered why and how God sent Christ, His Son, to die in our place so that we might be forgiven, Paul reminds us again that it was 'in accordance with the riches of God's grace'. This expands the idea of and underscores the importance of grace that we saw in verse 2 (see Day 5). In case we needed reminding, this emphasis on our salvation, our redemption, our being forgiven for our sins, has *nothing to do with our deserving it, but everything to do with His grace*, which He poured out on us. No wonder Paul praises the Father for having blessed us with every spiritual blessing in Christ! (1:3)

REFLECT AND RESPOND

- **Are you carrying any sense of guilt or shame today? Know that God did not intend for you to feel this way and pray that He will help you to move forward into the full benefits of being truly forgiven.**

- **Thank God for His amazing blessings on your life. You have been forgiven and redeemed. Thank Jesus for His incredible sacrifice.**

MEMORY VERSE

'Praise be to the God and Father of our Lord Jesus Christ, who has blessed us in the heavenly realms with every spiritual blessing in Christ.'

EPHESIANS 1:3

DAY 12

EXPECTANT

'he made known to us the mystery of his will according to his good pleasure, which he purposed in Christ, to be put into effect when the times reach their fulfilment – to bring all things in heaven and on earth together under Christ.' **EPHESIANS 1:9–10**

What are you expecting for the future? Are you expecting that life will get better or worse? Are you expecting promotion or demotion? Are you expecting your income to increase or decrease? Do you think the global economy will boom or go bust?

Here Paul is telling us that we can be *totally positive about the future.* This certainly wasn't because his immediate circumstances were particularly favourable or comfortable. Neither was it because he was simply a naive optimist denying present troubles and future challenges. Remember, he was actually writing from prison (see 3:1; 6:20) with no guarantee that he would be released. Rather, he is calling us to lift our gaze beyond our current situation, and to think long-term. In fact, to think very long-term, to the end of history. He is wanting us to focus our thoughts not on ourselves, other people or earthly rulers, but on God Himself and on His great future plan in Christ. Bishop Leslie Newbigin was once asked whether he was optimistic about a particular situation, and he replied: 'I am neither an optimist nor a pessimist. Jesus Christ is risen from the dead.' Paul's expectancy for the future was based on a similar confidence.

Why can he, and therefore we, be so confident about the future? Because God has graciously made known to us the mystery of His will. In the New Testament, this term 'mystery' generally means a previously hidden secret that has now been revealed. Through this letter and by the Holy Spirit, we are now given access to this secret, one that concerns not just our own future, but the future of the universe as a whole. And that's a secret worth knowing.

So what is this great mystery that has been revealed, and when will these things take place? Paul tells us that this will all happen when the times have reached their fulfilment. In Bible language this refers to the end of the first creation, or history as we know it, and to the beginning of the new creation and of our eternal future. This will take place when Christ returns, at which point God the Father will bring all things in heaven and on earth together under Christ, God's Son.

This glorious uniting of all things under Christ is at the core of Paul's expectancy for the future. The implication behind this passage is that not only were human beings alienated from God and from each other, but somehow the whole universe experienced some form of dislocation and division as a result of the Fall. The great promise here in Ephesians is that not only are we united with God in Christ, not only are we united together as Jewish and Gentile believers in Christ but somehow we are also going to be part of the unification of the *whole cosmos* in Christ. Through Christ, those who are part of God's new creation will live in a new heavens and earth, unified and living in the ultimate glory that God intended. This is truly wonderful and something to be very expectant about, regardless of whether you are a natural optimist, realist or pessimist. In recent British and American political history, we have experiences of new parties and leaders promising a brighter and better future, and being swept to power on the tidal wave of optimism, only for those hopes to quickly turn into disillusionment. However, for those of us in Christ, as far as the ultimate future is concerned, we can truly say that the best is yet to come, and it will be better than we can even imagine!

Right now, like the apostle Paul, you may be currently facing tough circumstances. It may be that you are facing personal and relational situations that seem fractured and divided. Of course, you can and should pray and believe God for breakthrough, and where possible, pursue relational reconciliation and unity in the immediacy of the present. But you can do so knowing that in the end, at the end of the age, Christ is coming back, and He is going to make all things new, unifying the universe under His loving Lordship, and we are going to be part of that glorious and perfect new creation forever!

REFLECT AND RESPOND

- **Have you experienced disappointment in the past that has made it hard for you to be hopeful of the future? Ask God to help you be expectant of good things to come.**

- **Look again at Ephesians 1:9–10, and spend a few moments thanking God that He has a plan to unite and perfect everything in Christ.**

MEMORY VERSE

'Praise be to the God and Father of our Lord Jesus Christ, who has blessed us in the heavenly realms with every spiritual blessing in Christ.'

EPHESIANS 1:3

INCLUDED

'In him we were also chosen, having been predestined according to the plan of him who works out everything in conformity with the purpose of his will, in order that we, who were the first to put our hope in Christ, might be for the praise of his glory. And you also were included in Christ, when you heard the word of truth, the gospel of your salvation.'
EPHESIANS 1:11–13

I don't know whether you have felt the pain of being excluded. I have – it was when I was about four! I distinctly remember playing with a group of friends, including some older children I idolised, only to find myself being excluded from the game. I was so distraught that I went home crying. My mum decided to sort the situation out and ensure that from then on I was included. (Don't worry, I have since had healing of the memories and I don't often cry – except in the run up to my daughters' weddings!)

If you have ever felt, or still do feel, somehow excluded, I have great news for you. You can know what it means to be included in Christ. That is the headline of today's passage. It helps if we understand that in these verses Paul is making a distinction here between himself and his fellow Jews ('we') and his Gentiles readers ('you'). Here he introduces one of the great themes of the letter, which is more fully unpacked in 2:11–3:13, which is that the Gentiles, who were previously excluded from God's purposes and God's people, are now included in Christ. Now, in Christ, each one of us can be included in God's great plan of salvation and are members of His eternal family.

Let's look at this in a bit more detail. First, from verse 11, Paul highlights the blessings that his fellow Jewish Christians have received. In what seems to be a recap and a re-emphasis of what he has said earlier in 1:4–5, he emphasises that their salvation was through God's initiative and grace, using words like 'chosen', 'predestined' and 'plan'. There is no doubt that Paul, once a persecutor of Christians, sees his inclusion in God's purposes as solely due to 'the plan of Him who works out everything in conformity with the purpose his will'. This doesn't mean that he or the other Jewish believers were mere robots. No, they responded to God's plan by being the first to hope in Christ. Their salvation, initiated by God and received by them, was 'for the praise of his glory'. Once again, we are reminded that Paul is not writing a theological tract, but a hymn of praise.

Having talked about himself and his fellow Jewish believers, he now turns to his Gentile readers and comes to his primary theme: they also were *included* in Christ. We will unpack this more fully in Week 5, but for now it is worth taking stock and recognising that this is a wonderful fulfilment of God's eternal plan. Throughout the Old Testament, the Jews were considered the people of God, with a mandate to be a light to the Gentiles, and with promises that one day the Gentiles, too, would be included. Here, through Christ and through Paul's ministry, the promises are being fulfilled. The Gentiles are now included!

How then are we included? It's as we hear the good news of Jesus Christ and what He has done for us that we can believe and receive His salvation. Moreover, it's as we share that news with others that they too can be saved and included!

This emphasis on inclusion goes straight to the heart of our need for belonging and helps answer one of our key questions: 'Where do I belong?' It highlights that salvation is not just individual but communal. One of the greatest privileges of becoming a Christian is that you and I get to *belong*, not just anywhere, but to the people of God, the family of God, the kingdom of God.

REFLECT AND RESPOND

- **Thank God for His sovereign plan: that through Christ, you have been included and that you now belong to the people of God.**

- **Thank God for the gospel, and ask Him to empower you to go and spread it so that others can be included, too!**

MEMORY VERSE

'Praise be to the God and Father of our Lord Jesus Christ, who has blessed us in the heavenly realms with every spiritual blessing in Christ.'

EPHESIANS 1:3

SECURE

'When you believed, you were marked in him with a seal, the promised Holy Spirit, who is a deposit guaranteeing our inheritance until the redemption of those who are God's possession – to the praise of his glory.' **EPHESIANS 1:13–14**

As our two daughters were growing up, one of my main goals as a dad was to help them feel secure. Somewhat imperfectly, I sought to show them that I loved them and that I would always be there for them.

Today we focus on how God, the *perfect* Father, has come to help us feel secure by giving us His 'promised Holy Spirit'. Throughout the Old Testament, God had promised to send His Spirit not just to special people like kings, prophets and priests, but to all His people (see Ezek. 36:26–27; 37:14; Joel 2:28–29). This promise was picked up by Jesus (Luke 24:49; Acts 1:4–5). Significantly, when Paul first went to Ephesus, one of the first things he did was to ensure that the disciples received this promised Spirit (see Acts 19:1–6).

In this passage in Ephesians 1:13–14, Paul highlights the Spirit's role in bringing security to all those who are in Christ. He uses two wonderful images to describe the Spirit. The first is that of a seal. At the time of Paul writing, seals would have been used in various ways, such as on cargo and documents. If, for example, a King wanted to send an important document he would write the letter, fold it over and secure it with his royal seal, signifying a mark of ownership and protection. This would let everyone know who this letter had come from, and would help ensure its safe delivery. When we believed the good news we were sealed with the Holy Spirit, which is God's way of telling us that we belong to Him, and that He will protect us in the trials of this life, right through to our eternal redemption in Christ.

The second picture of the Spirit is that of a 'deposit' or down payment. If, for example, you put down a deposit for a house or car, this is a guarantee of ownership and also promise of full payment at a later date. In the same way, Paul is saying that the Spirit is God's deposit and that God is our rightful owner – we can be totally secure that He is our Father and we are now His beloved children in Christ. Nothing is going to undo that fact. Moreover, not only is the Spirit the deposit guaranteeing the future, but He is also the first instalment of the future. It's as if we are enjoying right now something of our eternal inheritance, knowing that with certainty we will one day receive the fullness.

The use of the phrase 'guaranteeing our inheritance until the redemption of those who are God's possession' needs unpacking a little. While it could mean *our* inheritance, most commentators think it refers to us as *His* inheritance. If the latter, it means that we, who were chosen in Christ and predestined for adoption in eternity past and who were then redeemed and forgiven in history through the sacrifice of Christ, will, through the Spirit, ultimately be God's for the eternal future. Knowing that we are secure as His inheritance is the guarantee that we will enjoy our inheritance. As we shall see on Day 19, it's an inheritance like no other. We will be eternally rich!

So, how do we receive this promised Holy Spirit? First and foremost by believing and receiving the good news of Jesus. As we do, the Spirit comes into us and regenerates us – giving us new life, and making us new creatures in Him. Yet we don't have to stop there. As we see in Acts 19, there was clearly another dimension of the Spirit that was more akin to a baptism or infilling that came about when Paul laid his hands on the twelve men he found there, and resulted in them speaking in tongues and prophesying. But we mustn't stop there! Later in Ephesians 5:18, Paul exhorts us to 'be filled with the Spirit'.

The tense here indicates the need to 'go on being filled' or as the Amplified Bible puts it, 'ever be filled *and* stimulated with the [Holy] Spirit'.

REFLECT AND RESPOND

- **If you are not a Christian, but would like to be, then why not take time to invite Christ to come in and seal you for eternity with His Spirit.**

- **If you are a Christian, why not ask for more of His Spirit. Invite Him to fill and re-fill you, in Jesus' name!**

MEMORY VERSE

'Praise be to the God and Father of our Lord Jesus Christ, who has blessed us in the heavenly realms with every spiritual blessing in Christ.'

EPHESIANS 1:3

WEEK 2 ACTION STEPS

Look at the list of statements on Day 50 under Section 1, 'Identity' and allow them to take hold in your own life. Revisit this list as often as you can.

REFLECTION

Jot down anything that particularly spoke to you this week and anything you have discovered about your identity, belonging and purpose.

PRAYER

Is there anything you would like to thank God for or ask Him for? If you want, write your prayer down here. This can be a good way of being able to look back and see what God has done.

WEEK 3

PRAY FOR REVELATION

'For this reason, ever since I heard about your faith in the Lord Jesus and your love for all the saints, I have not stopped giving thanks for you, remembering you in my prayers. I keep asking that the God of our Lord Jesus Christ, the glorious Father, may give you the Spirit of wisdom and revelation, so that you may know him better. I pray also that the eyes of your heart may be enlightened in order that you may know the hope to which he has called you, the riches of his glorious inheritance in the saints, and his incomparably great power for us who believe. That power is like the working of his mighty strength, which he exerted in Christ when he raised him from the dead and seated him at his right hand in the heavenly realms, far above all rule and authority, power and dominion, and every title that can be given, not only in the present age but also in the one to come. And God placed all things under his feet and appointed him to be head over everything for the church, which is his body, the fullness of him who fills everything in every way.'

EPHESIANS 1:15–23 (NIV 1984)

PRAY WITH THANKSGIVING

'For this reason, ever since I heard about your faith in the Lord Jesus and your love for all the saints, I have not stopped giving thanks for you, remembering you in my prayers.' **EPHESIANS 1:15–16 (NIV 1984)**

If you are struggling with knowing how to pray, or want to grow in your prayer life, then this week's study should be hugely helpful. Years ago, when I was a new Christian, the main way that I prayed was by using the Lords' prayer. However, over the years, without neglecting to pray this way, I have come to realise and appreciate that there is a rich variety of ways to pray, and that some of the greatest prayers are contained in Paul's letters, especially here in Ephesians.

This week's passage, 1:15–23, is the first of two wonderful prayers, the second being 3:14–21. When I discovered these prayers of Paul I started praying them for myself, for other Christians and for other leaders. I would encourage you to start doing the same. Why? Because they are biblical prayers, and if they are in the Bible we can be confident that we will be praying in line with God's will.

Today, I want to emphasise that Paul starts his prayer with *thanksgiving*. One of the key lessons that I learned as I began to pray the Lord's prayer was the importance of first focusing on God and praising Him – 'Our Father in heaven, hallowed be your name' (Matt. 6:9) – before interceding and making requests. Paul prays a similar way. Remember that he has in effect started his whole letter with a tremendous hymn of praise to 'the God and Father of our Lord Jesus Christ' for having so blessed us with every spiritual blessing in Christ (1:3–14). Now he prays with thanksgiving to God for specific evidence of grace at work in the lives of his readers. In particular, he gives thanks for two things: for their 'faith in the Lord Jesus', and their 'love for all the saints', that is God's holy people. This is clearly not because either he or they are not facing any challenges! Rather, it is a deliberate posture that Paul adopts. In fact, he starts the majority of his letters with similar expressions of thanks, including in 1 Corinthians, to a church where there were major problems. It's as if he is choosing to celebrate what God has done and is doing in the lives of these early Christians as his starting point. Only then does he move to intercession and, where necessary, corrective teaching.

The fact that Paul had heard of their faith and love highlights that someone, somewhere, was telling stories of what God was doing in their lives. Over the years, I have been impacted by the importance of regularly telling and hearing stories of what God has done amongst His people. Having pastored one local church for over a quarter of a century there have been many situations along the way that have been a cause for concern or discouragement, but I can honestly say that my overall first response when I think of God's people is one of thanksgiving. Like Paul, I regularly pray for the church, and almost always I will start with thanksgiving.

This is important for a number of reasons. First, it glorifies God for what He has already done and is already doing in the lives of His people. Second, it changes us, because we focus on who we and our fellow believers are in Christ. Put simply, if we are thanking God for others, then it is hard to develop a bad attitude towards them!

So, we are to pray with thanksgiving, and we are also to pray *continually*. Paul was clearly a man who was devoted to prayer. Notice the language used here: 'I have *not stopped* giving thanks for you, *remembering* you in my prayers' (my emphasis). In our busy lives, how can we practice this lifestyle of prayer? In my own experience,

I have seen the value over the years of starting the day with prayer (and Bible reading), the blessing of praying 'in the Spirit' (Eph. 6:18) as well as the importance of praying with other people. Others, I know, find that having prayer lists are key to keeping disciplined: this helps them to remember who and what to pray for!

REFLECT AND RESPOND

- **Pray now, with thanksgiving, for those in your small group or your ministry team, as well as for the church as a whole.**

- **Make practical steps to remind yourself to pray these prayers regularly.**

MEMORY VERSE

'I keep asking that the God of our Lord Jesus Christ, the glorious Father, may give you the Spirit of wisdom and revelation, so that you may know him better.'

EPHESIANS 1:17

PRAY TO THE FATHER OF GLORY

'I keep asking … the God of our Lord Jesus Christ, the glorious Father' **EPHESIANS 1:17**

When our girls were little they quickly worked out that if they asked me for certain things in a certain way, they would often get what they asked! They were not being manipulative, and I wasn't spoiling them. It was just that they were my daughters and I was their devoted dad. Along similar lines, one of our church leaders recounted how his daughter came to him one Christmas and told him that she didn't want any presents but just wanted him to pay for her and several of her friends to go to New York for a holiday! Everybody laughs. But then he says that despite it being an audacious request, he doesn't even think to get angry with her for asking. In fact, if he actually had the resources to be able to fund the trip and knew that it was safe, he would want to do it. Why? Because he is her dad and he loves her. As good dads both of us want to give to our children what is good for them, within the limits of our resources.

When it comes to us praying to 'the God of our Lord Jesus Christ, the glorious Father', we can be even more confident, because He is both willing and able.

First, note that we pray to a Father who is *willing*. We don't come to any god but we come to a personal and loving Father God, who knows our needs and wants to answer our right requests – both our own and those that we pray on behalf of others. This God is both 'our Father' (1:2), and 'the God and Father of our Lord Jesus Christ' (1:3). It's worth pausing to dwell on this amazing fact that because we are in Christ, and because of our spiritual adoption (1:5), we now share in the relationship that Jesus Himself has with His Father, and that Jesus has now become our elder brother. What a privileged place we have in our new family and before the throne of God. We are not guests visiting, but family who belong there, and the Father says to us 'help yourselves'!

This emphasis on the centrality of God as Father was also at the heart of Jesus' teaching on prayer in the gospels. In Luke 11, for example, having taught His disciples to begin the Lord's prayer by saying 'Father' (11:2), He then goes on to use an example of how we are to be boldly persistent before God in prayer (Luke 11:5–10), before returning to the theme of the goodness of Father God, concluding with these stunning words: 'If you then, though you are evil, know how to give good gifts to your children, how much more will your Father in heaven give the Holy Spirit to those who ask him!' (Luke 11:13). In the parallel passage in Matthew's Gospel, it is clear that the Spirit is not the only gift that God gives: 'how much more will your Father in heaven give good gifts to those who ask him!' (Matt. 7:11). Note that, as a good Father, He will only give us what is truly good for us.

This means that as we come to God in prayer, we can come with boldness, knowing that He is a Father who is willing to answer our prayers. We can 'keep asking' for His Spirit to bring revelation and transformation in our lives and the lives of those we are praying for.

But there is a second dimension of the confidence we can have in prayer, and it's that God is also *able*. Not only is He described in 1:17 as 'the God of our Lord Jesus Christ' but also as 'the glorious Father' or better translated 'Father of glory' (ESV). The 'glory' of God refers to the splendour, brightness and power of His divine presence. This is surely Paul's way of reminding himself and us that we pray to a Father 'of glory', who is perfectly able to answer our prayers out of His limitless resources.

REFLECT AND RESPOND

- Whenever you pray, remember that you are speaking with your Father in heaven, who is both willing and able!

- Take time today to pray to your Father. You may want to pray the Lord's prayer or pray Paul's prayer here.

MEMORY VERSE

'I keep asking that the God of our Lord Jesus Christ, the glorious Father, may give you the Spirit of wisdom and revelation, so that you may know him better.'

EPHESIANS 1:17

DAY 17

PRAY FOR
THE SPIRIT'S HELP

'I keep asking that the God of our Lord Jesus Christ, the glorious Father, may give you the Spirit of wisdom and revelation, so that you may know him better. I pray that the eyes of your heart may be enlightened' **EPHESIANS 1:17–18**

Whilst I love reading paper books, being the owner of a Kindle has helped transform my reading experience. Not only does it mean that when I travel, I don't have to transport huge volumes around the planet, but it also means that I can read in the dark at night with the lights off. My old Kindle didn't have a built-in light, so I needed a cover with a light attached. My new one has a built-in light that illuminates the text. In both instances, having a light doesn't create the text – the text is there all the time. Rather, the light illuminates what is already there so that I can read and understand it.

Today we come to the heart of Paul's prayer in Ephesians 1, which is a prayer for spiritual illumination. He doesn't need to pray for the believers to be blessed – they already are, beyond measure (1:3–14). Instead, he prays that God will give them the Spirit of wisdom and revelation in order that their hearts may be 'enlightened', both so that they might know Him better, and that they might see how blessed they really are (1:18–19 – see Days 18–20).

Many years ago I heard a great story of a leading twentieth-century preacher who started praying Ephesians 1 (and the prayer in Eph. 3). He prayed for the Spirit of wisdom and revelation, and for his heart to be enlightened, and put himself as the subject of the prayer. He prayed it day after day for six months. At the time it didn't seem like much was happening, until suddenly the light started to come! He said that he started to grow far more than he had done in many years of his Christian life.

This illustration and this passage from Ephesians raise a number of questions. The first is: why do we need to ask for the Holy Spirit, when as Christians we have already been blessed with 'every spiritual blessing' (1:3), and have already received the Spirit as 'a deposit'? (1:13–14). The answer is because it is not enough just to have the Spirit in our lives. We need Him to actively show Himself to us, and for Him to come and help us by revealing spiritual truth (see John 14:26; 16:7–15).

The second question is: why do we need the Spirit to help us in this way, and why can't we see without the Spirit? Paul's answer is that before we became Christians we were darkened in our understanding and separated from the life of God (see Eph. 4:18). Even though, as Christians, we are now 'light in the Lord' (5:8), we still need the Spirit to reveal things to us because we are not talking about understanding natural truth but spiritual truth.

When Paul refers here to our need to 'know [God] better' he is writing from a Hebrew world-view, where 'knowledge' was not primarily about intellectual understanding, but was rather something personal and intimate. For us to know God in this way we need the Spirit's help. In 1 Corinthians, Paul puts this even more clearly: 'What no eye has seen, no ear has heard, and what no human mind has conceived – the things God has prepared for those who love him – these are the things God has revealed to us by His Spirit. The Spirit searches all things, even the deep things of God. For who knows the thoughts of God except the Spirit of God. What we have received is not the spirit of the world, but the Spirit who is from God, so that we may understand what God has freely given us.' (1 Cor. 2:9–12). There's so much we could say about this wonderful passage. Put simply, Paul is saying that we can't know God or what He has prepared for us through our natural senses, but we can know Him through the revelation that His Spirit brings us. We can see through the Spirit's illumination.

REFLECT AND RESPOND

- **Follow Paul's example and start praying this prayer for yourself and others – that the Father would give you the Spirit of wisdom and revelation so that you may know Him better!**

MEMORY VERSE

'I keep asking that the God of our Lord Jesus Christ, the glorious Father, may give you the Spirit of wisdom and revelation, so that you may know him better.'

EPHESIANS 1:17

PRAY TO KNOW THE HOPE OF HIS CALLING

'I pray that the eyes of your heart may be enlightened in order that you may know the hope to which he has called you' **EPHESIANS 1:18**

We all need hope. Viktor Frankl, survivor of Auschwitz and Dachau and author of the famous book *Man's Search for Meaning*, tells how hope was the single most important factor in surviving in the camps – even more important than physical health. He tells the story of one man who was convinced they would be liberated by Christmas. This hope kept him alive and positive for months. However, when Christmas came and went and they weren't liberated, he simply curled up and died. When a prisoner lost hope, said Frankl, 'he lost his spiritual hold'. [9]

Paul recognised the importance of hope. Hence, here in 1:17–19, having first prayed that the Spirit would help us know God better, he then prayed for us to be enlightened in order that we might know how much God has blessed us and planned for us. In particular, he prayed that we would know the hope of His calling, the riches of His inheritance (see Day 19) and the greatness of His power (see Days 20–21). He starts first with 'the hope to which he has called you'.

As we have already seen on Day 12, this biblical hope is not the vague, semi-optimistic type of hope, epitomised by the term, 'I hope so!' Rather, this hope can be translated as a confident expectation for the future – a hope that is based on something solid and sure and that concerns God's plan to unite the whole redeemed cosmos in and through Christ (Eph. 1:9–10).

But it is one thing for us to have reasons for hope, it is another to actually know this so that it affects the way we think and live. Hence, here in 1:17–18, Paul prays for us to receive the Spirit of wisdom and revelation so that our hearts might be 'enlightened' concerning the hope of our calling. The fact that our hope is not based on our optimistic outlook but on God's calling on our lives is hugely reassuring. The 'calling' refers back to God's plan, which stretches back to eternity past. His calling includes the fact that He chose us in Christ before the creation of the world (1:4). It includes the fact that He predestined to be adopted as His children (1:5). It includes the fact that in history He sent His Son to shed His blood that we might be redeemed and forgiven (1:7–8). It includes the fact that at a point in time we heard the gospel, believed and received the promised Holy Spirit as a seal and a deposit, guaranteeing His and our future inheritance (1:13–14). If God has thus called us, we can have a sure hope – a confident expectation for what's to come.

This is tremendously encouraging. Right now you and other believers around you may be facing tough, temporary circumstances and you are not sure what the outcome will be. Yet you can be filled with a great hope, knowing that your future is based on *His* calling and that calling will never fade or fail. Even in the middle of trials you can experience great joy, because you know that in spite of the battle, the ultimate war has been won, and that we will enjoy the eternal rewards of His victory for and in us.

This is all true, and yet Paul knew that we need help to *know* this. So he prayed, as we must pray – both for ourselves and others – that the Spirit of wisdom and revelation would so flood our innermost being with light that we might see the hope of our calling, and that this might change the way we view the future.

REFLECT AND RESPOND

- Take time today to pray this wonderful prayer of Ephesians 1:17–19, both for yourself and for others.

- This week, continue to ask God for revelation concerning the hope of His calling. As you keep on praying this way, expect that your heart and the hearts of those you are praying for will be enlightened to know the hope of His calling.

MEMORY VERSE

'I keep asking that the God of our Lord Jesus Christ, the glorious Father, may give you the Spirit of wisdom and revelation, so that you may know him better.'

EPHESIANS 1:17

PRAY TO KNOW THE RICHES OF HIS INHERITANCE

'I pray that the eyes of your heart may be
enlightened in order that you may know …
the riches of his glorious inheritance in the saints'
EPHESIANS 1:18 (NIV 1984)

It's a great tragedy to be rich and never know it. Let me illustrate with
a couple of stories:

There was a report in a newspaper of a homeless man in rural
Wyoming who was wearing only a light jacket when he died from
hypothermia. Even more tragically, it was discovered that he was in fact
the heir to a great fortune; he was a relative of a multimillionaire, who
died leaving an estate valued at $306.5 million, of which $19 million
was due to this homeless man. How tragic to die of the cold, and yet
be heir to such a massive fortune.[10]

I heard another true story of a man who inherited some money
and decided to invest it in a farmhouse in Portugal. He saw the house
on the internet and arranged a viewing. On the day of the viewing
it was pouring with rain, so he decided not to go down to the barn
at the bottom of the property. He then made the offer, bought the
farmhouse, moved in and after a couple of days decided to look at

the barn. The door was welded shut. So he cut the latch off and peered through the gloom to find row after row of amazing classic cars, worth £12.6 million!

The great news is that for those who are in Christ, we have far greater riches than this. As we have already seen (1:3–14), these riches have been made available to us by grace and we did nothing to deserve them. They have come to us through Christ and His sacrificial death. They are now made available to us through the 'Holy Spirit, who is a deposit guaranteeing our inheritance' (1:14). Here, Paul is praying that we would experience the Spirit's help so that we might realise how blessed we really are. Why? Because, like the stories above, it is very possible to be a Christian, to have a vast inheritance, but either never know it, or live like we've forgotten it.

As we saw before (Day 14), there is a debate as to whether this is talking about God's inheritance in us, or our inheritance, but in real terms it points to the same thing – especially to our future inheritance of which our present experience of the Spirit is a foretaste. So what is this rich inheritance that Paul is eager for us to know about? There's lots we could say about this because the Bible has a lot to say, but for now, let me summarise by looking at three aspects.

First, there is the promise of a new, resurrected body. The great news for the Christian is that death is not the end, but a temporary separation from the body as we await the return of Christ. When He comes back, we will receive new bodies in the likeness of His resurrection body. Paul describes it like this: 'our citizenship is in heaven. And we eagerly await a Saviour from there, the Lord Jesus Christ, who, by the power that enables him to bring everything under his control, will transform our lowly bodies so that they will be like his glorious body' (Phil. 3:20–21).

Second, there is the promise of a new home. When Christ comes back He will renew creation and bring it into its eternal glory, and it will become our eternal home. Listen to these hugely encouraging words: 'in keeping with his promise we are looking forward to a new heaven and a new earth, where righteousness dwells' (2 Pet. 3:13).

Third, there is the promise of a new glory as God comes in person to live with us on the new earth: 'God's dwelling place is now among the people, and he will dwell with them. They will be his people, and God himself will be with them and be their God. "He will wipe away every tear from their eyes. There will be no more death" or mourning or crying or pain, for the old order of things has passed away' (Rev. 21:3–4).

No wonder Paul prayed that we might *know* all this!

REFLECT AND RESPOND

- **Take time to thank God for the riches of His inheritance.**

- **Pray for yourself and others concerning a greater revelation of this inheritance.**

MEMORY VERSE

'I keep asking that the God of our Lord Jesus Christ, the glorious Father, may give you the Spirit of wisdom and revelation, so that you may know him better.'

EPHESIANS 1:17

PRAY TO KNOW THE GREATNESS OF HIS POWER, PART 1

'I pray … that you may know … his incomparably great power for us who believe. That power is the same as the mighty strength he exerted when he raised Christ from the dead' **EPHESIANS 1:18–20**

Occasionally, there are news reports of unexploded bombs from the Second World War being found. At other times, people go about their business, sometimes walking their dogs over fields where bombs are hidden, with children inadvertently playing with the bombs, all the while quite unaware of the sheer power that is so close to them.

Christians can be a little bit like that – completely unaware of the power that is already theirs. Notice here that Paul doesn't pray that God would give them more power (although he does pray for a manifestation of that power in his second prayer in Eph. 3), but he first prays that God would give them a revelation of the power that they already have.

Power and victory is an important theme throughout this letter, especially given the culture of Ephesus and its surroundings. For example, in the ruins of this ancient city there is a surviving stone carving of the Greek goddess Nike, the goddess of victory (hence the use of the name by a sports brand). To believers in Ephesus who were once dominated by such evil and victorious powers (2:2) and who still faced a battle against these powers (6:12), Paul is concerned that they know they are on the winning side and that God's power in and through them is far greater than any power they have been freed from or will face. As if to emphasise this, he uses four different Greek words for power to highlight the enormity of God's power that is available to the Church: *dunamis* (from which we get our word dynamite), *energia* (mighty working), *kratos* (might) and *ischuos* (strength). This is the 'incomparably great power' that is available for Christians then and now!

This revelation of the power that we have is not just theory, but is vital for our Christian living. For example, you may be struggling with a sin and you don't think you have the power to overcome. Or you want to share the good news with others in word and deed, but feel lacking in power. But here Paul would say to us: you already have a power that is greater than any other. Then he goes on to demonstrate why this is so. It is because the power that is at work in our lives is the *same power* that raised Christ from the dead. Think about this: Jesus was clinically dead and had been buried in a tomb for three days, when God the Father released His power and raised Him from the dead, in the words of Peter on the Day of Pentecost, 'freeing him from the agony of death, because it was impossible for death to keep its hold on him' (Acts 2:24). Remarkably, Paul is saying that this same death-defeating, grave-overcoming power is at work in our lives as Christians. It's a power unlike any other and greater than any other. I love the Amplified Bible translation of this Ephesians passage: Paul prays for our eyes to be opened by the Spirit: ['so that you can know and understand] what is the immeasurable *and* unlimited *and* surpassing greatness of His power in *and* for us who believe, as demonstrated in the working of His mighty strength, Which He exerted in Christ when He raised Him from the dead and seated Him at His [own] right hand in the heavenly [places]' (1:19–20). Notice the piling on of these adjectives

– the immeasurable, unlimited and surpassing greatness of His power both *in and for us who believe.*

Given the greatness of God's power that is available to us, and the fact that so often we live in ignorance of this power, it is no wonder that Paul makes a revelation of this power central to his prayer here in Ephesians 1. There are few prayers that are more vital for us to pray: that we might grasp by revelation, God's 'incomparably great power for us who believe.'

REFLECT AND RESPOND

- **Pray this marvellous prayer for yourself, for those in your local church and for all Christians everywhere. Pray that as we walk in the revelation of this great power, our lives we be changed, and we will go out and change the world!**

MEMORY VERSE

'I keep asking that the God of our Lord Jesus Christ, the glorious Father, may give you the Spirit of wisdom and revelation, so that you may know him better.'

EPHESIANS 1:17

PRAY TO KNOW THE GREATNESS OF HIS POWER, PART 2

'That power is the same as the mighty strength he exerted when he raised Christ from the dead and seated him at his right hand in the heavenly realms, far above all rule and authority, power and dominion, and every name that is invoked, not only in the present age but also in the one to come. And God placed all things under his feet and appointed him to be head over everything for the church, which is his body, the fullness of him who fills everything in every way.' **EPHESIANS 1:19–23**

Yesterday we looked at the high point of Paul's prayer in 1:15–23, which concerned the 'incomparably great power for us who believe' (1:19), a power which is the same power that raised Christ from the dead. This is such a hugely important point that Paul doesn't stop there, but unpacks this more fully by looking at four different aspects of God's power in Christ. As we look at each of these, remember Paul's purpose, which is to emphasise the greatness of His power that is available for us!

First, God's power raised Christ from the dead. Why did Paul use the resurrection rather than other great biblical events such as creation to speak about God's power available to us? Partly because he will go on to liken our salvation to a resurrection from the dead (Eph. 2:4–5). But partly, surely, because in Christ overcoming death, and therefore all the powers of sin and death, He overcame the greatest opposition to the will and love of God. If sin and death couldn't hold Christ, then it can't hold us! What could be of greater comfort and confidence to us as Christians to know that the power that is working in us is a power that will ultimately overcome all opposition, including, at the end of the age, death itself?

Second, God's power exalted Christ to His right hand. It is so important that we don't stop at the resurrection, as central as this is, but move on to an understanding of the ascension (see Acts 1:9–11). Through the resurrection, we can say that Christ *lives* forever. Through the ascension we can say that Christ *reigns* forever. Here, Paul is emphasising Christ's exaltation and authority above all things, including evil powers. In fact, He has been exalted 'far above all rule and authority, power and dominion, and every name that is invoked' not only in the present age but also in the one to come. Since we are seated with Him in the heavenly realms, we can spiritually share in His reign now (see Eph. 2:5–6 and Day 24).

Third, God's power brought everything under subjection to Christ. That means everything good and evil is under His rule. How are we to explain this when we look at our world today? Christians often use a World War Two analogy. On D-Day, 6 June 1944, the Allies successfully landed on the Normandy beaches. We now know, with the benefit of hindsight that, especially with the Russians advancing in the east, this opening of a second front effectively meant that Hitler was defeated. But there were another eleven months of some of the bloodiest fighting before the war was finally over on VE Day, 8 May 1945. In the same way, Christ has already won the decisive battle, the enemy is effectively defeated, but we are now in the in-between time, knowing that victory *is assured*.

Fourth, Christ rules over all things for the *benefit of the Church*. Here, Paul highlights the remarkable union of Christ and His people, with Him described as the Head and us as His Body, 'the fullness of him who fills everything in every way' (1:23). The fact that we are now part of Christ and that He fills us as His Body is indeed a wonderful mystery, with staggering implications. It means that if Christ now rules over all things in these in-between times, and we are united to Him as a body is to its head, then we can be fully confident that in the middle of a battle we have all the power we need, because of our union with Him!

As we pray, may the Lord give us increasing revelation of the incomparable greatness of His power that is available to us. And may we be filled with great confidence as a result!

REFLECT AND RESPOND

- **Take time to ponder the incomparable power of Christ and rejoice in the fact that this power is at work in you!**

- **Use the whole of Ephesians 1:15–23 to pray for yourself and others today.**

MEMORY VERSE

'I keep asking that the God of our Lord Jesus Christ, the glorious Father, may give you the Spirit of wisdom and revelation, so that you may know him better.'

EPHESIANS 1:17

WEEK 3 ACTION STEPS

1. Go to Day 50, Section 4, 'Prayer' and contemplate the prayer promises.

2. Write out Ephesians 1:17 on a piece of card or somewhere easy to access, such as by the phone. Use it to pray for yourself, your family, friends and members of your small group and church family.

REFLECTION

Jot down anything that particularly spoke to you this week and anything you have discovered about your identity, belonging and purpose.

PRAYER

Is there anything you would like to thank God for or ask Him for? If you want, write your prayer down here. This can be a good way of being able to look back and see what God has done.

WEEK 4

ALIVE FOR HIS PURPOSE

'As for you, you were dead in your transgressions and sins, in which you used to live when you followed the ways of this world and of the ruler of the kingdom of the air, the spirit who is now at work in those who are disobedient. All of us also lived among them at one time, gratifying the cravings of our flesh and following its desires and thoughts. Like the rest, we were by nature deserving of wrath. But because of his great love for us, God, who is rich in mercy, made us alive with Christ even when we were dead in transgressions – it is by grace you have been saved. And God raised us up with Christ and seated us with him in the heavenly realms in Christ Jesus, in order that in the coming ages he might show the incomparable riches of his grace, expressed in his kindness to us in Christ Jesus. For it is by grace you have been saved, through faith – and this is not from yourselves, it is the gift of God – not by works, so that no one can boast. For we are God's handiwork, created in Christ Jesus to do good works, which God prepared in advance for us to do.'

EPHESIANS 2:1–10

DAY 22

SAVED FROM
THE DEPTHS

'As for you, you were dead in your transgressions
and sins, in which you used to live when you
followed the ways of this world and of the ruler of
the kingdom of the air, the spirit who is now at work
in those who are disobedient. All of us also lived
among them at one time, gratifying the cravings of
our flesh and following its desires and thoughts.
Like the rest, we were by nature deserving of wrath.'
EPHESIANS 2:1–3

This week in 2:1–10, we will be looking at the amazing transformation
that takes place when someone becomes a Christian, a change that
involves being spiritually raised from the dead and being seated with
Christ in heavenly places. However, looking at the good news of our
spiritual resurrection in 2:4–7, we need to first understand the state
we were in before we came to Christ, which is the main focus of 2:1–3.

In life, we often describe how bad things used to be before telling
the good news. I find myself doing this when I recount stories of how
God has healed people. For example, a lady responded to a word
of knowledge in a meeting and came out with a large goitre on her
neck. The good news is that having been prayed for, it shrank and
then almost completely disappeared. As I told the KingsGate church

family about this story, I found myself emphasising the goitre first, and then telling about how God had healed her. So dramatic was this healing that many of her community started coming along, and they, too, started getting healed. Similarly, we heard a story of a lady in Peterborough who had been healed of a tumour and cancerous spots. As she told her story on video, she described her condition before recounting with joy what God had done for her, and how her whole life and future had been transformed as a result.

It's the same when it comes to our spiritual salvation. Sometimes we need to be reminded of the condition we were in before God rescued us. Here at the start of chapter 2, Paul starts by graphically portraying how bad things were before we were saved, before going on to dramatically and joyfully portray how our lives have been transformed in Christ.

He starts with a simple but stark statement: 'you were dead in your transgressions and sins'. Clearly he can't be talking about physical death, but about spiritual death, which is a way of describing our condition before we came to Christ – as separated from the life of God and being unable to know Him or respond to Him.

Then he goes on to highlight what this spiritually dead life looked like and how we were enslaved to three forces, which can be summarised as the world, the devil and the flesh.

First, we were enslaved by 'the ways of this world'. The world here doesn't mean the physical earth, but the present world system that is dominated by a culture and philosophy that rejects its Creator and His ways.

Second, we were enslaved by 'the ruler of the kingdom of the air, the spirit who is now at work among those who are disobedient'. In other words, we were not just dominated by a humanistic anti-God system but rather influenced by a spiritual force of evil, elsewhere known as the devil, who hates God, and us as human beings, who are made in God's image.

Third, we were enslaved as we went around 'gratifying the cravings of our flesh and following its desires and thoughts'. We can't just blame the world and the devil but rather must recognise that it was our own sinful nature (literally the flesh) that caused us to go our selfish way rather than God's way, with all the destructive consequences that followed. It is not just that we are those who sinned. It is rather that we were sinners by nature, with an inner propensity to do bad things.

As if to make the point, Paul is saying that this is not just the condition of a few particularly depraved individuals or societies, but it included all of us. The result was not just bad for us, but it affected our relationship with a righteous and holy God, and as a result we were 'by nature deserving of wrath'. This is not something we tend to think about, but it highlights that while intensely loving, God is steadfastly opposed to evil and its destructive forces. Therefore, before we came to Christ we were under His judgment and wrath.

This 'bad' news only serves to emphasise how 'good' the good news is!

REFLECT AND RESPOND

- **If you became a Christian at an early age, thank God for what He has saved you from.**

- **If you became a Christian later in life, take some time to remember what you were like before you became a Christian. Thank God for what He has done in your life.**

MEMORY VERSE

'And God raised us up with Christ and seated us with him in the heavenly realms in Christ Jesus'

EPHESIANS 2:6

DAY 23

RESCUED

'But because of his great love for us, God, who is rich in mercy, made us alive with Christ even when we were dead in transgressions – it is by grace you have been saved.' **EPHESIANS 2:4–5**

In October 2010, the world watched and celebrated as 33 Chilean miners were safely rescued from their collapsed mine. An explosion 69 days earlier had left the men stranded 5 kilometres below ground. In their helplessness they had started daily prayer meetings, led by a committed Christian named Jose Henriquez, during which time a number of the miners also committed their lives to Christ. Some time after their deliverance, Henriques began travelling around telling the story. On one occasion, at Dallas Baptist University, when the chapel crowd rose to their feet to give him an ovation, he said: 'Please don't give me praise. The glory goes to Jesus Christ. He is the one who accomplished this.'[11]

In our text today, the apostle Paul starts to unpack the story of a far greater rescue, in fact the greatest rescue in history, which concerns our spiritual salvation. There are a number of comparisons and contrasts with the story of the miners. First, like them, we were helpless to save ourselves. But unlike them, our condition was far worse. If the miners could have found an escape route they would have climbed out, whereas, as Paul reminds us again, we were spiritually dead in our sins and transgressions and therefore totally incapable of making our way out in any condition. Second, like the miners, we have experienced an amazing transformation. For them, the contrast between being buried underground for 69 days, with finally being rescued and brought up and out into the light, was tremendous. But our transformation was even more dramatic since it is likened here to a resurrection from death to life. Third, like Henriquez, we can rightly give the glory to God for our salvation. But unlike the miners, who prayed to God but were rescued by fellow ordinary human beings, our deliverance is totally from God, through His one and only Son, Jesus Christ, and the only perfect human being capable of rescuing us through His sacrificial death on the cross.

Yet, no matter how wonderful what God has done in rescuing us, Paul's emphasis here is more on *why* God did it. In this passage, 2:4–10, Paul keeps highlighting the wonder of God's motivation in saving us, using four key words – 'mercy', 'love', 'grace' and 'kindness' – with the first three of these mentioned here in 2:4–5. The frequency of these words serves to highlight that our salvation was because He desired it, not because we deserved it.

First, God is described as being 'rich in mercy'. Mercy is normally associated with help for the desperate or helpless. He saw us in our helpless state, unable to save ourselves, and He came to rescue us.

Second, God was motivated because of His great love for us. This word 'love' is the Greek word *agape*, which is the unconditional, unselfish love that is concerned for the good of the other. Paul wants us to know that it was out of His great love, not our loveliness, that He saved us. This, by the way, means that we can be assured of His ongoing love towards us, because He *is* love!

Third, God rescued us because of His grace. Grace is already something that was emphasised in chapter 1 (1:2; 1:6–7). Now in this short section it is referred to two times (2:5; 2:8). It's so important for our understanding that we have already considered it on Day 5, and will look at it again on Day 26. For now though, it's enough to emphasise that our salvation was a free gift and nothing to do with the fact that we deserved it or earned it.

This really is the greatest rescue act in history. Even when we were dead, God made us alive with Christ. Why did He do it? Because of his great love, mercy and grace.

REFLECT AND RESPOND

- **Think about the wonder of God's salvation; think about His rich mercy, great love and free grace towards you.**

- **If you don't know Christ, invite Him to save you.**

- **If you do know Him, pray for opportunities to tell others about this greatest rescue act in history.**

MEMORY VERSE

'And God raised us up with Christ and seated us with him in the heavenly realms in Christ Jesus'

EPHESIANS 2:6

RAISED UP AND SEATED WITH CHRIST

'And God raised us up with Christ and seated us with him in the heavenly realms in Christ Jesus, in order that in the coming ages he might show the incomparable riches of his grace, expressed in his kindness to us in Christ Jesus.' **EPHESIANS 2:6–7**

Imagine you are sitting in a plane on a runway. As the plane starts to take off and reaches its desired altitude of over 30,000 feet above the clouds, you too are flying high above the clouds. Now, if you were asked: 'Are you going up?' You would say 'yes'. If you were asked: 'Are you flying high?' You would say 'yes'. But it is not so much that you are flying as that the plane is flying and you are going up and flying high because you are in the plane!

In today's passage, Paul uses the two phrases 'with Christ' and 'in Christ' to make a similar point; that what happened to Christ has happened to those who are in Christ. In verse 5, we saw that God made us alive with Christ. Here Paul takes things a stage further: 'And God raised us up with Christ and seated us with him in the heavenly realms in Christ Jesus' (2:6).

This marvellous theme is a continuation of Paul's prayer in 1:19– 20: a prayer that we might know God's 'incomparably great power for us who believe' and how that power was the same power that 'he exerted when he raised Christ from the dead and seated him at his right hand in the heavenly realms'. Having shown us how staggering the power of God was in Christ, to raise Him 'from the dead and [seat] him at his right hand' (1:20), here in 2:5–6 Paul returns to our being raised up with Him. We were not just rescued from spiritual death, but were raised up and seated with Christ. Why? Because when we believed the gospel, God did the greatest miracle of all. He placed us *in* Christ. Just as in the analogy of the plane, whatever happened to Christ automatically happened to us!

This clearly needs some unpacking and pondering. What could it mean for us to be raised up and seated with Christ? Although elsewhere, such as in 1 Corinthians 15, Paul tells us that in the future we will share in Christ's physical resurrection, here he is telling us something very different. This is not a future event but something that has already happened, and therefore is something that we are living in *right now*! So, rather than this being about physical resurrection, this is talking about the spiritual resurrection of all believers. Just as we were spiritually dead, when we accepted Christ we were made spiritually alive with the same power that raised Him.

But it's even more wonderful than that. Not only are we now alive and raised up, but we are also *seated with Him* in the heavenly realms. Again, this is not talking about us being physically present with Him – we will have to wait for the end of the age when Christ comes back and we receive our new bodies. But the truth is nonetheless real – we have been made alive and made to sit with Christ in the heavenly realms 'far above all rule and authority, power and dominion' (1:21). This is not so much about us being seated 'up there', as if heaven is spatially above us, but is about us being exalted with Christ in a position of *authority* over negative spiritual forces. So, we are now no longer to be negatively fearful or dominated by spiritual powers that may have once enslaved us. Rather, in a restoration of the mandate in Genesis 1 (see the Introduction), but now in an even greater way, we are called to positively rule with Christ from a spiritual altitude that is far higher than 30,000 feet!

We are now seated with Christ in heavenly places, and in His name we can come boldly before God's throne in prayer, and can minister boldly to people, because we now share Jesus' position of authority. Quite amazing!

God did all this, making us alive and seating us with Christ, not because we deserved it, but because of His mercy, love, grace and kindness towards us. This not only means wonderful blessings in this life, but expressions of His kindness towards us 'in the coming ages'. Throughout eternity we, as His redeemed people, will be displayed as trophies of His grace.

REFLECT AND RESPOND

- **What a privilege to be raised up and seated with Christ. As I write this, my heart is so full of gratitude towards Him. Join me in praising God for the incomparable riches of His grace.**

MEMORY VERSE

'And God raised us up with Christ and seated us with him in the heavenly realms in Christ Jesus'

EPHESIANS 2:6

SAVED BY GRACE
THROUGH FAITH

'For it is by grace you have been saved, through faith – and this is not from yourselves, it is the gift of God – not by works, so that no one can boast.'
EPHESIANS 2:8–9

Imagine two doors. One is marked 'our works', the other 'God's grace through faith'. Many people keep trying the first door in a vain attempt to be saved, before finally trying the second door and entering in by God's grace through faith. This was Martin's story. Born 10 November 1483 in Eisleben, Saxony, he grew up with the prospect of becoming a lawyer, before ending up as a monk, largely due to a morbid fear of God and a desperate desire to earn his salvation. On occasions, he fasted so much he would faint, and at other times he would engage in self-flagellation. He spent so long in confessing his sins that his confessors told him not to come back until he had something worth confessing! Looking back on this phase of his life, he commented drily: 'If ever a monk could have got to heaven by monkery, it would have been me'.[12] A turning point came when he realised that Paul's emphasis on the righteousness of God was not so much God's judgment against sin, but rather God's free gift of righteousness that was available to all who put their trust in Jesus. When he made the discovery that salvation was by grace through faith, apart from works, he said: 'thus I felt as if I was born again; as if I had found the Gates of Paradise wide open to me'.[13]

The man in question was Martin Luther, one of the key leaders of the sixteenth-century Reformation, which was one of most important movements in history. Up until that point, the medieval Church had built, over a number of centuries, a very elaborate system of how people might be able to gain acceptance with God through various good deeds, a system that Luther was particularly dedicated to. Following his conversion and his revelation of grace, Luther and other Reformers started diligently studying their New Testaments and preaching from Paul's writings, in particular. One of their favourite passages was in Ephesians 2:8–10, where Paul unpacks the relationship between grace, faith and our good deeds. It is such an important section that we will look at verses 8–9 today, and verse 10 for the next two days.

Grace, a word which has often been summarised as 'God's Riches At Christ's Expense' is something that we have already looked at in Days 5 and 23. However, the fact that once again it receives such a prominent position is worth reflecting on. Here grace, or unmerited favour, is clearly used in contrast to works or merited favour to highlight that we could do nothing to deserve or earn God's favour. As if to underscore this, Paul adds: 'this is not from yourselves, it is the gift of God'. By now, I trust that this is obvious: our salvation is a *gift*, the greatest gift available to man. This marks out Christianity from all other religions and philosophies.

So what then of faith? We have already looked at the subject of faith on Day 3. Here Paul makes clear that faith is not so much about us doing something – for that would undermine grace – rather, faith is about us receiving what God has given to us in Christ. Faith is about us *trusting* in God for what He has done for us in Christ.

This is such a key revelation. I remember that, for me personally, it was some while after I had become a Christian before I really grasped this. Although I had been saved by grace, was radically converted and experienced genuine life change, in practice in my thinking and actions, I often lived as if what I *did* was the key to God's ongoing acceptance of me. That was until I was in a Bible study at university when I had a revelation that my right standing with God was gift, and that my salvation was wholly from His grace through faith.

In summary, we are saved by grace through faith. This, as the Reformers were so keen to emphasise, rules out the role of good works in our acceptance before God. To be a Christian is no cause for boasting or pride at all, because it is all of God and all of grace.

REFLECT AND RESPOND

- **Take time today to thank God once more for His gift of salvation. Hold out your hands to receive more of His grace through faith.**

MEMORY VERSE

'And God raised us up with Christ and seated us with him in the heavenly realms in Christ Jesus'

EPHESIANS 2:6

HIS WORKMANSHIP

'For we are God's workmanship, created in Christ Jesus to do good works, which God prepared in advance for us to do.' **EPHESIANS 2:10 (NIV 1984)**

I occasionally like going to art galleries. I remember on one occasion when Karen and I visited the National Gallery in London. There was a one-off exhibition, a unique opportunity to see two of Van Gogh's famous *Sunflower* paintings side by side. We queued for what seemed ages – I thought it was an hour – Karen assures me it wasn't and I wouldn't queue for an hour for anything! We finally went into this little room that simply had these two paintings. We studied them for a short while and then we left! The question is, why did we, along with thousands of others each day, decide to queue for so long to view these two paintings? Because of *who painted them*! If they had been Dave Smith's *Sunflowers*, no one would have gone. But they were Van Gogh's *Sunflowers* and as such they were priceless masterpieces.

Today, we are focusing on the glorious truth that we are 'God's workmanship, created in Christ Jesus'. This word 'workmanship' has the sense of being a poem, work of art or masterpiece – something of exquisite design and wonder. The glorious truth is that we are God's Masterpiece, His greatest work. That makes us *hugely valuable*. Realising this is key to understanding our new identity and is worth meditating on!

So, how, given that before we came to Christ, our lives are often inwardly very flawed and are far from being pleasing to God, can

Paul say that we are 'God's masterpiece'? The answer lies in the next phrase: 'created in Christ Jesus.' This word 'created' is linked to the original creation idea of God making something completely new (see Gen. 1–2), and refers to our new birth in Christ. Just as God was immensely pleased with His first creation and made humankind the crown of this original creation, so now in Christ we are made new creations, in fact, the crown of His new creation. The great twentieth-century preacher Martyn Lloyd-Jones summarises the significance of this: 'What is creation? The very idea, the essential idea, is that something is made out of nothing; it was not there before, but it is now brought into being. That is the precise way in which the apostle thinks of the Christian. So we must say farewell forever to all ideas of improvement, and of self-improvement especially. The most important fact about the Christian is that he is a new creation, a new creature. God the Creator, God the Potter, the Artificer, God the great Maker, the great Workman, has brought something into being in my life that was not there before – that is what makes me a Christian.'[14]

For me personally, this revelation of being a new creation was one of the most transformational experiences in my early Christian life. I remember memorising and meditating on a similar verse to Ephesians 2:10. It was 2 Corinthians 5:17, 'Therefore, if anyone is in Christ, the new creation has come: the old has gone, the new is here!' The more I meditated on this verse, the more I realised what a miracle God had done in me. I had been completely transformed from the inside out. The more I realised how much God had done in making me a brand new creation, the more it felt natural for me to live the new life that He had given me. It's not that I have never struggled in my Christian life, but the combination of a powerful work of the Spirit in my conversion, and this revelation from the Bible that I was a brand new creation meant that I felt free to love God, and serve Him as the number one priority in my life. The same is true for you. If you are in Christ, you are a new creation, God's masterpiece. He has transformed your life for ever, for your good and for His glory!

This highlights the importance of us knowing our new identity (we are 'God's workmanship, created in Christ Jesus') as the foundation to us fulfilling our new purpose (doing 'good works, which God prepared in advance for us to do.')

REFLECT AND RESPOND

- **If you are a Christian, take time to reflect and thank God for who He made you to be. Declare over yourself: 'I am now God's workmanship, His masterpiece, His new creation in Christ.'**

- **If you are still seeking, why not ask Christ to come in and make you brand new?**

MEMORY VERSE

'And God raised us up with Christ and seated us with him in the heavenly realms in Christ Jesus'

EPHESIANS 2:6

GOOD WORKS

'For we are God's handiwork, created in Christ Jesus to do good works, which God prepared in advance for us to do.' **EPHESIANS 2:10**

One of the greatest rescues in history was at Dunkirk in early 1940. The British and their allied troops of over 330,000 men had been forced back to the beaches of Dunkirk, a small town in France. They waited for what seemed like their inevitable destruction. However, the British managed to mobilise a flotilla of boats and sent them across the English Channel in the face of great danger in an attempt to evacuate the stranded troops. By the ninth day, a total of 338,226 soldiers had been rescued. It is a stirring story, but what is interesting is the speech that Winston Churchill made to the Commons following the rescue: 'we must be very careful not to assign to this deliverance the attributes of a victory. Wars are not won by evacuations.'[15] In other words this was a great rescue but there was still a war to fight. Churchill was not in any way trying to underestimate the magnitude of the rescue; he was reminding the people of Britain that they had rescued their troops in order that they might continue to fight for victory. They were rescued for a purpose!

Jesus achieved an even more miraculous and greater rescue for us than the rescue from Dunkirk. And we must be ever grateful. But we should also remember that Jesus rescued us for a purpose. This emphasis on being rescued for a purpose was one of the reasons why Ephesians 2:8–10 was one of the favourite passages of the sixteenth-century Reformers. Verses 8–9 (which we looked at yesterday) enabled them to steer away from the legalistic salvation by works emphasis of much of the medieval Church. Verse 10, on the other hand, helped them to bring correction in the face of those who began to teach what is sometimes called 'cheap grace', and assisted them in re-emphasising the right place of good works in the life of a true Christian. Martin Luther came up with a pithy statement: 'Good works don't make a good man, but a good man does good works.'[16] In other words, we are not saved *by* our works, we were saved *for* good works, 'which God prepared in advance for us to do'.

So, what are these good works? In Week 6 we will consider the idea of the specific calling or purpose that God has for each of us. But the verse here implies a more general concept that every Christian has been set apart for a life of doing good. This includes the big issues, like helping to alleviate poverty and human suffering, to bring justice and help to the marginalised, and to preach the good news and see the Church of Jesus Christ grow and prosper throughout the earth. But it also includes more everyday activities. It is significant that Paul uses the language of new creation here – we are God's workmanship, *created* in Christ Jesus. Part of our mandate as new creations is to help steward this old creation in preparation for co-ruling with Christ in the new heavens on the new earth! This creational theology is integral to a biblical world-view and means that there should be no such distinction between secular and sacred works. Rather, every good work we do in and through Jesus Christ is sacred. Stacking the dishwasher and doing the gardening are part of the good works that we have been called to!

So, too, are ordinary workplace activities, like being a fair and just employer or a hard-working and diligent employee. In Ephesians 4–6, Paul unpacks some of these more ordinary lifestyle good works. In the parallel letter to the Colossians, he summarises this new attitude to our works: 'whatever you do, whether in word or deed, do it all in the name of the Lord Jesus, giving thanks to God the Father through him' (Col. 3:17).

REFLECT AND RESPOND

- **What are some of the good works that God has called you to do in your home, your place of work or your neighbourhood?**

- **Ask God to help you live your life for His glory.**

MEMORY VERSE

'And God raised us up with Christ and seated us with him in the heavenly realms in Christ Jesus'

EPHESIANS 2:6

DAY 28

THE WONDER
OF SALVATION

As I look around at the Christians who seem to be most happy, effective and fulfilled, it seems that they have one thing in common: they have never got over getting saved! This was certainly the case with the apostle Paul. He never ceased to be amazed at the kindness of God in rescuing him. The result? A life of gratitude and sacrificial service. In this week's stunning passage, Ephesians 2:1–10, Paul seeks to impress on his readers a wonderful reminder of what God has done for us in Christ. So, as we come to the conclusion of this week, I want to encourage you to re-read this whole passage slowly and out loud, pondering on the wonder of your salvation.

'As for you, you were dead in your transgressions and sins, in which you used to live when you followed the ways of this world and of the ruler of the kingdom of the air, the spirit who is now at work in those who are disobedient. All of us also lived among them at one time, gratifying the cravings of our flesh and following its desires and thoughts. Like the rest, we were by nature deserving of wrath. But because of his great love for us, God, who is rich in mercy, made us alive with Christ even when we were dead in transgressions – it is by grace you have been saved. And God raised us up with Christ and seated us with him in the heavenly realms in Christ Jesus, in order that in the coming ages he might show the incomparable riches of his grace, expressed in his kindness to us in Christ Jesus. For it is by grace you have been saved, through faith – and this is not from yourselves, it is the gift of God – not by works, so that no one can boast. For we are God's handiwork, created in Christ Jesus to do good works, which God prepared in advance for us to do.' **EPHESIANS 2:1–10**

There are a number of key truths to remember and rejoice in.

First, if you are a Christian, it's good to remember what you were saved *from*. Remind yourself that before Christ rescued you, you were dead in your sins and transgressions: you were enslaved to the world, the devil and your own sinful nature. And as a result, you were under God's wrath. Just as a jeweller might present to you a diamond ring on a black cloth to show the brilliance of the jewel, so, too, Paul is showing the wonder of our salvation in contrast to the darkness of our life without Christ.

Second, it's good to remember who you were saved *by*. The simple answer is by God and by Him alone. You were spiritually helpless and yet in His mercy, love, grace and kindness He came and rescued you, and made you alive in Christ.

Third, it's good to remember *how* you were saved. The simple answer is: through Christ and in Christ. You came into union with Him, and as a result you share in His victory, His resurrection and His ascension. Now, amazingly, you are alive *in Him*, and are seated *with Him* in heavenly places. Now that you are in Him, you are God's workmanship, you are God's glorious new creation.

Fourth, it's good to remember what you were saved for. Although you were not saved *by* your good works, you were saved *for* good works. This means that you are called to live a life that is pleasing to God and honouring to Him.

This truly is the greatest rescue ever!

REFLECT AND RESPOND

- **Spend some time praising God for the wonder of your salvation.**

- **Why not take the time to write our your own salvation story and look for opportunities to share that story with others?**

MEMORY VERSE

'And God raised us up with Christ and seated us with him in the heavenly realms in Christ Jesus'

EPHESIANS 2:6

WEEK 4 ACTION STEPS

1. Revisit the list of declarations on Day 50 under Section 1, 'Identity' and take them to heart.

2. If you want to become a Christian, follow this prayer, focused around three key words: admit, believe, commit. You can pray this on your own, or you can ask another Christian to pray with you: 'Lord Jesus, I admit my need of You and invite You to come and forgive me today. I believe that You died and rose again so that I could receive new peace, hope, joy and purpose. Please come into my life today. I commit to follow You all the days of my life. Amen!'

3. If you have already come to Christ, take some time to think about and write out your own story of how God has changed your life. Think about what you were like before you became a Christian, what happened when you became a Christian and in what way being a Christian has impacted you.

4. Ask God to give you an opportunity to share your story with someone this week and for the boldness and confidence to make the most of it.

REFLECTION

Jot down anything that particularly spoke to you this week and anything you have discovered about your identity, belonging and purpose.

PRAYER

Is there anything you would like to thank God for or ask Him for? If you want, write your prayer down here. This can be a good way of being able to look back and see what God has done.

WEEK 5

BELONGING TO HIS FAMILY

'Therefore, remember that formerly you who are Gentiles by birth and called "uncircumcised" by those who call themselves "the circumcision" (which is done in the body by human hands) – remember that at that time you were separate from Christ, excluded from citizenship in Israel and foreigners to the covenants of the promise, without hope and without God in the world. But now in Christ Jesus you who once were far away have been brought near through the blood of Christ. For he himself is our peace, who has made the two one and has destroyed the barrier, the dividing wall of hostility, by setting aside in his flesh the law with its commandments and regulations. His purpose was to create in himself one new humanity out of the two, thus making peace, and in one body to reconcile both of them to God through the cross, by which he put to death their hostility. He came and preached peace to you who were far away and peace to those who were near. For through him we both have access to the Father by one Spirit. Consequently, you are no longer foreigners and aliens, but fellow citizens with God's people and members of his household, built on the foundation of the apostles and prophets, with Christ Jesus himself as the chief cornerstone. In him the whole building is joined together and rises to become a holy temple in the Lord. And in him you too are being built together to become a dwelling in which God lives by his Spirit.'

EPHESIANS 2:11–22

FAR OFF AND BROUGHT NEAR

'Therefore, remember that formerly you who are Gentiles by birth and called "uncircumcised" by those who call themselves "the circumcision" (which is done in the body by human hands) – remember that at that time you were separate from Christ, excluded from citizenship in Israel and foreigners to the covenants of the promise, without hope and without God in the world. But now in Christ Jesus you who once were far away have been brought near through the blood of Christ.' **EPHESIANS 2:11–13**

In a 1944 lecture at the University of London, C.S. Lewis reflected on the universal human desire to be included and to fit in. He called the object of this mysterious craving the 'Inner Ring'. He said, 'I believe that in all men's lives at certain periods, and in many men's lives at all periods between infancy and extreme old age, one of the most dominant elements is the desire to be inside the local Ring and the terror of being left outside.'[17] He was highlighting that all of us have an inherent need for *belonging*.

One of the great themes of Ephesians is that in and through Christ, we now *belong to the family of God*. This has been hinted at in 1:2 and

1:11–12 (see Days 4 and 13), but now takes centre stage in 2:11–22 and is the main focus of this week's study.

In the text above we see that Paul is celebrating the fact that the Gentiles, who were once far off, have now been brought near. But before he gets to their inclusion in verse 13, he reminds them of their exclusion in verses 11–12.

Talking of exclusion, one of the most sobering moments of my rebellious teenage years was when two of my best friends were excluded from school. Providentially, I was on holiday with my family, while they spent a night wrecking the garden of one of our least favourite teachers. As a result, both of them were excluded from our highly prestigious school, one temporarily, the other permanently. It was an awful day for them, and I can't imagine how potentially devastating it would have been for me to have joined them in their exclusion.

Here, Paul is reminding Gentile Christians of their previous exclusion from the people of God. They were not excluded through bad behaviour, but rather by birth, that is by being born Gentiles. Therefore, they were outsiders who failed to receive the covenant mark of circumcision, and thus were labelled derogatorily by the Jewish insiders as 'the uncircumcised' and 'dogs'. Then he encourages them to remember what this state of being on the outside looked like. First, they were separated from Christ, the Messiah. Second, they were excluded from being God's chosen people, Israel. Third, they were foreigners to the covenants that God had made with His people. Fourth, they were therefore without ultimate hope for the future. Fifth, they were without the one true God. In the words of one commentator they were 'Christless, stateless, friendless, hopeless and Godless.'[18] Paul summarises this in verse 13 by saying simply that they were 'far away'.

This was not only true for the Gentile Christians back then, it is true for every single one of us today. We were born not just sinners, but outsiders. However, there is a wonderful 'but'! Just as in 2:4 we read the words, 'But … God', so now in 2:13, we read '*But now* in Christ

Jesus you who were once far away have been brought near through the blood of Christ' (my emphasis).

The sense of being brought near highlights that we who were *excluded* have now been fully *included*. Why? Because we are now in Christ Jesus. It is because we are in Christ that we are near to God and are included in the people of God. How? Not because of our own efforts or worthiness, but because of 'the blood of Christ'. This reference to Christ's blood highlights that are we reconciled to God because of His atoning sacrifice. But it also points the way to 2:14–18, where Paul emphasises that now, through Christ, Gentile Christians are united together with Jewish Christians in a new covenant of grace. More of that tomorrow!

REFLECT AND RESPOND

- **Think about the wonderful privilege of belonging to the family of God.**

- **Thank God that though you were once excluded, now in Christ, you are fully included.**

MEMORY VERSE

'And in him you too are being built together to become a dwelling in which God lives by his Spirit'
EPHESIANS 2:22

RECONCILED

'For he himself is our peace, who has made the two one and has destroyed the barrier, the dividing wall of hostility, by setting aside in his flesh the law with its commandments and regulations. His purpose was to create in himself one new humanity out of the two, thus making peace, and in one body to reconcile both of them to God through the cross, by which he put to death their hostility. He came and preached peace to you who were far away and peace to those who were near.' **EPHESIANS 2:14–17**

There is a deep longing within humanity for peace and reconciliation. On Christmas Eve and Christmas Day 1914, during arguably the most devastating war in history, German and British soldiers entered into 'no man's land', where they laid down hostilities for a period to come together, talk to each other and engage in burial ceremonies for the deceased war casualties. Troops from both sides were also friendly enough to play games of football with one another, with several gatherings ending with carol singing. This moving story of the Christmas truce points to a short period when the barrier, the dividing wall of hostility, was temporarily removed. Sadly, the fighting and hostility soon resumed and the world as we know it was changed forever.

Sometimes in history a more permanent wall is removed. I remember visiting Berlin in the late 1980s, a city divided since 1961 by the Berlin Wall. After a few days experiencing the colourful opulence of West Berlin, with its high life and economic prosperity, it was a shock to go across into East Berlin. Life on the other side was heavily policed, very drab, and obviously much poorer. A few months later the historic divisions were symbolically ended as the Wall was demolished and Germany was reunified.

An even more dramatic and altogether more significant event took place in c.AD 30, ensuring the possibility of universal, eternal peace and reconciliation. As Jesus Christ died a sacrificial death on the cross, He first and foremost re-established peace between God and man (see Day 6). The first three Gospels record how, as Jesus breathed His last, the curtain separating the Holy Place was torn in two, thus symbolising that the way to God was now open.

But here in Ephesians 2:14–17, the emphasis is on Jesus dying to bring peace and reconciliation between human beings, particularly between Jew and Gentile. He destroyed the barrier, the dividing wall of hostility.

What was this barrier? Perhaps the simplest explanation is that it was the division created within the Temple by the Law. The Temple in Jerusalem was at the very centre of the worship and faith of Israel, but it also contained many gates and walls. It separated the activity of the high priest from the other priests, the priests from the people, the Jewish men from the women, and the Jews from those furthest away, the Gentiles. Jesus destroyed these historic divisions, not through a physical act of pulling this wall down, but as we read in our passage, 'by setting aside in his flesh the law with its commandments and regulations.' This means that good and holy as the Law was and is, it excluded those outside the Law and failed to provide salvation for those who try to keep it (see Gal. 3:10–14). Now, in Christ, this barrier has been removed, and there is a new way to get saved that is available to all, Jew and Gentile alike.

All of this means that now through the cross, Christ has dealt a death blow to the division between Jew and Gentile, creating one new race or one new people in Christ, encapsulated in this wonderful phrase 'one new humanity.' In Galatians 3:28, Paul highlights that this ending of racial and religious divisions extends to those of class and gender.

'There is neither Jew nor Greek, neither slave nor free, nor is there male and female, for you are all one in Christ Jesus.' All those who are in Christ get to be part of this new race.

At KingsGate, the church I pastor, one of our great delights is that God has blessed us with many different nations, united in one family. To celebrate our diversity we occasionally have International Evenings – where we bring our national dishes for everyone else to taste and enjoy. Many come in their national dress, and after filling ourselves with great food from different nations, we will often sing and dance together. Without erasing national distinctiveness, we are in effect rejoicing together in the fact that we are 'one new humanity in Christ'.

REFLECT AND RESPOND

- **Take time to thank God for the reconciliation that He has made available in Christ.**

- **Pray for people and places in the world torn apart by fighting and division, that the good news of Christ might be proclaimed and that the peace of God might rule and reign.**

MEMORY VERSE

'And in him you too are being built together to become a dwelling in which God lives by his Spirit.'
EPHESIANS 2:22

ACCESS TO GOD

'For through him we both have access to the Father by one Spirit.' **EPHESIANS 2:18**

Imagine if you were suddenly given 24/7 access to the ruler of your nation, which meant that at any time of the day or night, you could come to him or her and ask for anything that was in their will and power to grant. Wouldn't that be a great privilege? Well, today we are considering something more wonderful, which is the privilege of 24/7 eternal access to God the Father, Creator of heaven and earth, King of kings and Lord of lords!

With the Old Testament tabernacle and Temple, it was quite clear that there was very restricted access to God's presence, which was assumed to be at the very heart of the structure. The Holy of Holies or Most Holy Place was a small inner sanctuary, separated from the rest of the Temple by a curtain. Access was only granted to one person, the high priest, and only to him, once a year on the Day of Atonement. On the other side of the curtain, in what was known as the Holy Place, only a separate, special group of people, the priests, were allowed to enter. Then, as we saw yesterday, there were separate courts for the Jews, the women and finally the Gentiles. Yet here we read something staggering. Now *all* of God's people, Jews and Gentiles, are granted *permanent access* into the very presence of God. This is so wonderful that it needs unpacking, since this incredible privilege was only made possible through the involvement of the whole Trinity.

First, notice that God is described as the 'Father'. Earlier in this passage we are reminded that Gentiles were 'without God' (2:12), and that we were reconciled 'to God through the cross' (2:16). But here the language changes from us being reconciled to *God* to having access to the *Father*. This again highlights what we saw in Day 10: that the highest privilege we have of all is to be adopted as children, and to enjoy the closest and deepest possible relationship with our Father in heaven.

Second, this access is only possible through Christ. The simple phrase 'through Him' contains a whole theology of redemption (see eg Day 11) and helps explain how we now have access to the Father that was not available to those under the old covenant. There is much we could say here, but it is worth reminding ourselves that we have access because of Jesus as both our sin-bearer and our great High Priest. The sacrifices that the Old Testament priests had to do, day after day, are no longer needed because of the once-and-for-all sacrifice of Christ on the cross (see Heb. 10). Moreover, Christ is also our High Priest who has opened the way for us, and is now at the right hand of the Father, interceding for us and guaranteeing our living access. It is worth quoting the momentous words of Hebrews 10:19–22, which unpacks more fully the magnitude of our access: 'Therefore, brothers, since we have confidence to enter the Most Holy Place by the blood of Jesus, by a new and living way opened for us through the curtain, that is, his body, and since we have a great High Priest over the house of God, let us draw near to God with a sincere heart in full assurance of faith' (NIV 1984).

Third, this access to the Father, through Christ Jesus, is only possible by the Spirit. Paul's use of the phrase 'one Spirit' is yet again his way of emphasising that since there is only one Spirit, there is only one people of God and only one way that we together enter His presence. Why do we need the Holy Spirit to give us this access? Because the Spirit is the presence of God here on the earth. He is the One who comes to live in us, regenerate us, fill us and give us the spirit of adoption by which we cry '*Abba*, Father' (see Rom. 8:15). Elsewhere, we learn that worship is by the Spirit (see John 4:23–24; Eph. 5:18–20), and that we are to pray in the Spirit (see 1 Cor. 14:13–14; Eph. 6:18–20).

REFLECT AND RESPOND

- **Why not take some time right now, or set aside time later in the day, to come before this amazing God? Worship the Father, through Christ, by the Spirit. Enjoy His presence!**

MEMORY VERSE

'And in him you too are being built together to become a dwelling in which God lives by his Spirit.'

EPHESIANS 2:22

A CITIZEN OF GOD'S KINGDOM

'Consequently, you are no longer foreigners and strangers, but fellow citizens with God's people'
EPHESIANS 2:19

Over the next few days we will continue to explore this wonderful theme of belonging by exploring three different concepts that Paul unpacks in Ephesians 2:19–22: we are citizens of God's people, members of God's family and a part of God's temple. Today, we will be looking at the first of these, which is the amazing privilege we have of being *citizens of God's kingdom*.

Many people are living in countries other than where they were born, and years on, still feel very much like outsiders. Even if they have lived in their new country long enough to enjoy all the privileges and responsibilities of citizenship, often they sadly feel like they don't really belong. However much they try, there still seems to be a distinction between living in a country based on a passport rather than through a birth certificate.

Here, Paul, using the language of being part of a city or state, is keen to emphasise that those of us who were formerly Gentiles, born outside God's kingdom, are now no longer foreigners and strangers but are 'fellow citizens with God's people'. In the words of Martyn Lloyd-Jones: we 'no longer live on a passport, but … we have our birth certificates … we really do belong'.[19] Following Lloyd-Jones' lead, let me highlight something of what this means.

First, we are a people who are separated from, and made distinct from, all others. Ancient cities had a wall around them to separate the citizens from the outsiders. We, as citizens of God's kingdom, have been separated from the world, not in the sense that we no longer live in it, but as those who are set apart for God and protected from the 'evil one' (see John 17:11–19).

Second, we are a people who are bound together by a common allegiance. We all acknowledge the same Head, and we have common interests.

Third, we have amazing privileges. The greatest of these is that we have our King! Most nations have some sort of ruler, be it a monarch, a prime minister, a president or another grand title – some people like their nation's political system, others less so. We, as the people of God, have a King who is the 'King of kings, and the Lord of lords'.

Fourth, we have a capital city. Many nations pride themselves on their capital city – Rome, London, Paris, Washington. But we have a capital, a headquarters, that is far greater – heaven itself. Elsewhere, Paul puts it this way: 'But our citizenship is in heaven' (Phil. 3:20).

Fifth, we have fellow citizens. One of the huge blessings of being in Christ is that we are now part of a worldwide eternal kingdom, and we belong with billions of fellow citizens – past, present and future – in God's kingdom and before His throne.

Finally, we also have the privilege of looking ahead to the future glory of that kingdom. While right now we are *spiritually* connected to God in heaven through Christ and the Spirit, there is coming a day when we will be *physically* united with our King and with His kingdom. As Paul continues in Philippians 3: 'And we eagerly await a Saviour from there, the Lord Jesus Christ, who, by the power that enables him to bring everything under his control, will transform our lowly bodies so that they will be like his glorious body' (Phil. 3:20–21).

All of this highlights the wonderful privilege of being 'citizens of God's kingdom'. In Christ we are no longer a foreigner: we now belong!

REFLECT AND RESPOND

- As you go about your normal business in this world, try to stop every now and then to remind yourself that you are a citizen of another kingdom, the kingdom of heaven, and recall the wonderful privileges that you have as a result.

MEMORY VERSE

'And in him you too are being built together to become a dwelling in which God lives by his Spirit.'
EPHESIANS 2:22

DAY 33

A MEMBER OF
GOD'S FAMILY

'Consequently, you are no longer foreigners and
strangers, but … members of his household'
EPHESIANS 2:19

Yesterday we looked at the huge privilege of being a citizen of
God's kingdom. Here, Paul moves on to talk of something even
more wonderful and intimate: the fact that we are *members of
God's family*.

When my youngest brother was adopted (see Day 10), he
immediately became a full member of our family. From day one, the
fact that he was adopted didn't seem to matter at all. As an older
brother, I loved him, played with him, and as he grew up, I argued,
wrestled and bantered with him, as if he were my natural younger
brother. Why? Because from the moment he was adopted, he became
as much a part of the family as the rest of us.

In the same way, Paul is saying to all of us who are Gentiles that
we are now 'no longer foreigners and strangers' but are now God's
children – members of 'God's household'. This term 'household'
refers to the extended family that is still present in many non-Western
cultures. The wonderful news is that there is a family, God's family,
and we get to be full members of it.

How is this possible? As have seen throughout our study, it is by
being 'in Christ', specifically by being 'adopted' as God's children

(see Eph. 1:5). Not only does this mean that God is now our Father, and that the Lord Jesus is now our elder brother, but that we now belong to God's worldwide, eternal family, the Church. This is a huge privilege. But it is not enough just to rejoice in our belonging to the *universal* Church, we need to experience and live out this belonging in the context of a *local* church. Most of Paul's letters were written to *local* churches. Although Ephesians was most likely a circular letter written to a number of churches, Paul's practical instructions in chapters 4–6 assumes that, even here, he expects his readers to live in unity and work out responsibilities within the context of the local church family.

This is so important. Sadly, some Christians use the excuse of being part of the universal Church, not being part of a local church. Others, while officially part of a local church, are so in name only and give or receive very little to living out their privileges and responsibilities as family members. In his book *The Purpose Driven Life*, Pastor Rick Warren highlights the need to be committed to a local church family and writes: 'Today's culture of independent individualism has created many spiritual orphans – bunny believers, who hop around from one church to another without any identity, accountability, or commitment. Many believe you can be a good Christian without joining (or even attending) a local church, but God would strongly disagree.'

Rick then gives a number of reasons why you need a church family:
- 'A church family identifies you as a genuine believer. You are not the body of Christ on your own.'
- 'A church family moves you out of self-centred isolation. The local church is a lab for practicing unselfish, sympathetic love.'
- 'A church family helps you develop spiritual muscle. You will never grow to maturity just by attending worship services and being a passive spectator. Only participation in the life of a local church builds spiritual muscle.'
- 'The body of Christ needs you. God has a unique role for you to play in His family.'

- 'You will share in Christ's mission in the world. The church is God's instrument on Earth.'
- 'A church family will help keep you from backsliding. In the church, we receive the encouragement of others to stay on track, as well as the protection of spiritual leaders.'[20]

All of this highlights some of the privileges and responsibilities of belonging to God's family.

REFLECT AND RESPOND

- **Which one of these points in Rick Warren's list most speaks to you?**

- **If you are not fully committed to and actively involved in your local church, take steps to get more connected!**

MEMORY VERSE

'And in him you too are being built together to become a dwelling in which God lives by his Spirit.'
EPHESIANS 2:22

A PART OF HIS TEMPLE

'built on the foundation of the apostles and prophets, with Christ Jesus himself as the chief cornerstone. In him the whole building is joined together and rises to become a holy temple in the Lord. And in him you too are being built together to become a dwelling in which God lives by his Spirit.'
EPHESIANS 2:20–22

A turning point came in my own life when I started at Oxford University and someone invited me to a church in the centre of the city. Although I didn't particularly connect with the service as a whole, something happened to me as we sang the final hymn. As I joined in the singing, I suddenly become aware of a living, loving presence right there beside me. I literally started trembling in what I quickly realised was the presence of God. What had happened? By being in the presence of Spirit-filled Christians worshipping, I encountered the God who, by His Spirit, was dwelling in and amongst His people.

This is what Paul wants to emphasise here. Having highlighted the wonder of us being citizens in God's kingdom and members of God's family, he goes on to give us a third picture, which is our inclusion as part of God's own temple, where He Himself dwells by His Spirit.

Throughout the Bible – from the idea of creation as a temple for God's glory, to Moses' portable tabernacle, to Solomon's magnificent Temple and the rebuilt second Temple – the Temple was central to the aspirations of God's people. By the time of the Christian era, the idea of a 'new temple' as the symbol of Israel's restoration became linked to hopes for the coming of the Messiah. Other ideas had already begun to surface, including the idea of a heavenly temple coming down to earth, the concept of the community of the faithful as a spiritual temple and the Greek idea of man as a temple.

Against this backdrop, Paul, in his earlier letters to the Corinthians (see 1 Cor. 3:16 and 2 Cor. 6:16–7:1), introduced the revolutionary idea that now God's Spirit dwells in His people collectively, with the added emphasis that the body of the individual believer is now the temple of the Spirit (see 1 Cor. 6:19). N.T. Wright highlights how radically shocking this idea was. He writes, 'The magnitude of Paul's transformed symbolic world becomes at once apparent. "You are the temple of the Living God", he says: not to the Philippians he loved so much, not to the Thessalonians in the midst of their suffering and danger, but precisely to the recalcitrant, muddled, problem-ridden Corinthians. This is not, in other words, a sober judgment based on the noticeable holiness, or gospel inspired love or joy, of this or that ekklesia church. It is simply for Paul, a fact: the living God, who said he would put his name in the great House in Jerusalem, has put his name upon and within these little, surprised communities, dotted about the world of the north east Mediterranean. Unless we are shocked by this, we have not seen the point.'[21]

Here in his later letter to the Ephesians, in 2:20–22, Paul continues and develops these ideas from the Corinthian letters. First, he introduces the notion of the apostles and prophets as the foundation of this new building. Then he highlights that the distinctiveness of this new temple is that Christ Jesus is the chief cornerstone, meaning that all is built on Christ, supported by Christ, and the shape of the continuing building is determined by Christ, the cornerstone.

Then Paul re-emphasises the key point that this new Jew-Gentile race of people is now being made into a building, a temple where God lives by His Spirit. It is worth pausing here to consider the enormity of this. The Church is the place where the omnipresent God dwells in a particular way, and will manifest Himself.

This should cause our expectancy to rise every time we gather in His name – be it twos or threes (see Matt. 18:20), in a small group, or larger meetings. As we do so, the God who lives in and amongst us as His people will manifest Himself to those around. Many, like me in that church in Oxford, will sense His living, loving touch and will begin a journey of transformation.

REFLECT AND RESPOND

- **Take time to re-read and think over on this week's memory verse.**

- **Ponder on the fact that the Church is the temple of God, the place where God dwells by His Spirit, and you are called to be part of this.**

MEMORY VERSE

'And in him you too are being built together to become a dwelling in which God lives by his Spirit.'
EPHESIANS 2:22

THE WONDER OF BELONGING!

'Therefore, remember that formerly you who are Gentiles by birth and called "uncircumcised" by those who call themselves "the circumcision" (which is done in the body by human hands) – remember that at that time you were separate from Christ, excluded from citizenship in Israel and foreigners to the covenants of the promise, without hope and without God in the world. But now in Christ Jesus you who once were far away have been brought near through the blood of Christ. For he himself is our peace, who has made the two one and has destroyed the barrier, the dividing wall of hostility, by setting aside in his flesh the law with its commandments and regulations. His purpose was to create in himself one new humanity out of the two, thus making peace, and in one body to reconcile both of them to God through the cross, by which he put to death their hostility. He came and preached peace to you who were far away and peace to those who were near. For through him we both have

access to the Father by one Spirit. Consequently, you are no longer foreigners and aliens, but fellow citizens with God's people and members of his household, built on the foundation of the apostles and prophets, with Christ Jesus himself as the chief cornerstone. In him the whole building is joined together and rises to become a holy temple in the Lord. And in him you too are being built together to become a dwelling in which God lives by his Spirit.'
EPHESIANS 2:11–22

Here in this passage, we find the answer to the big life question, 'Where do I belong?' If you are a Christian, the resounding answer is: 'I now belong to the people of God, the kingdom of God, the family of God and the temple of God'.

What this means practically is that as amazing as our *individual* salvation is, there is a *communal* dimension to us being in Christ. So let's step back and remind ourselves of the key truths in this week's study.

First, where were we before we came to Christ? Paul's answer is that we were *excluded*. As Gentiles (unless you happen to be of Jewish descent), we were the 'uncircumcised', 'separate from Christ, excluded from citizenship in Israel and foreigners to the covenants of the promise, without hope and without God in the world' (2:12).

Second, where are we now? Paul's stunning answer is that we have now been *included* in the people of God, no longer divided, but united in one new humanity or race in Christ. We are a brand new community who have been reconciled and 'brought near' to God and to one another through Christ and His cross. We now have joint access to the very presence of the Father, through the Spirit. No longer is this access to a holy God restricted to one man, once a year, but now there is unlimited access to God our Father, 24/7.

As this new people of God we now have tremendous privileges: we are now 'fellow-citizens' with God's people'; we are 'members of God's household', with God as our Father, Jesus as our elder brother and all Christians as our brothers and sisters; we are part of God's temple, 'being built together to become a dwelling in which God lives by His Spirit'.

Third, where will we be in the future? Together in Christ forever! The kingdom that we are part of is an eternal kingdom, the family that we are in will last forever, and the temple that we are part of has yet to be finished. The fact that we are 'being built together' implies that there is a work that is still to be done in this life, and that this work will only be finally complete in the life to come. In this age and in this life, God dwells with us by His Spirit. In the age to come and in the new creation, heaven will come to earth, the Father and the Son will dwell with us and we will 'see his face' (Rev. 21:3; 22:4). What a glorious day that will be!

REFLECT AND RESPOND

- **Take time to praise God for the wonder of belonging to His family.**

- **If you are not yet vitally connected to a local church, take steps to rectify this: God has a place where you can belong!**

MEMORY VERSE

'And in him you too are being built together to become a dwelling in which God lives by his Spirit.'

EPHESIANS 2:22

WEEK 5 ACTION STEPS

1. Look at the list of declarations on Day 50 under Section 2, 'Belonging' and really take them on board.

2. Make a decision to get connected and stay connected to the local church. Think about how practically you can get more involved both in and through a small group and through weekend services.

REFLECTION

Jot down anything that particularly spoke to you this week and anything you have discovered about your identity, belonging and purpose.

PRAYER

Is there anything you would like to thank God for or ask Him for? If you want, write your prayer down here. This can be a good way of being able to look back and see what God has done.

WEEK 6

GIFTED FOR SERVICE

'For this reason I, Paul, the prisoner of Christ Jesus for the sake of you Gentiles – Surely you have heard about the administration of God's grace that was given to me for you, that is, the mystery made known to me by revelation, as I have already written briefly. In reading this, then, you will be able to understand my insight into the mystery of Christ, which was not made known to people in other generations as it has now been revealed by the Spirit to God's holy apostles and prophets. This mystery is that through the gospel the Gentiles are heirs together with Israel, members together of one body, and sharers together in the promise in Christ Jesus. I became a servant of this gospel by the gift of God's grace given me through the working of his power. Although I am less than the least of all the Lord's people, this grace was given me: to preach to the Gentiles the boundless riches of Christ, and to make plain to everyone the administration of this mystery, which for ages past was kept hidden in God, who created all things. His intent was that now, through the church, the manifold wisdom of God should be made known to the rulers and authorities in the heavenly realms, according to his eternal purpose that he accomplished in Christ Jesus our Lord. In him and through faith in him we may approach God with freedom and confidence. I ask you, therefore, not to be discouraged because of my sufferings for you, which are your glory.'

EPHESIANS 3:1–13

A CALLING FROM GOD

'For this reason I, Paul, the prisoner of Christ Jesus for the sake of you Gentiles – Surely you have heard about the administration of God's grace that was given to me for you' **EPHESIANS 3:1–2**

This week, in Ephesians 3:1–13, we are going to be focusing on the third of our big life questions: 'What am I living for?' This concerns the huge issue of each of us knowing our life *purpose*. We looked more broadly at our overall purpose on Days 3 and 27. This week, by looking at Paul's own example, we are going to be looking at our specific purpose, calling and life assignment.

Knowing and fulfilling the specific purpose and calling for my own life has certainly been one of the most important aspects of my spiritual journey. As I look back to before I became a Christian, I would characterise my life as lacking a sense of overall and ultimate purpose. The day that I accepted Christ, I was filled with a deep sense that God had a purpose for me to fulfil. Over the years, as I have listened to Him, sought the counsel of others, and have tried to be faithful to following His path for me, I have had increasing clarity on the specific assignment that He has given me. The clearer I have become in this, the more freeing it has been.

Here in Ephesians 3:1–13, we can see a number of aspects of Paul's own calling that, while unique, we can also apply to our own lives, starting here in verses 1–2. First, notice the weightiness of God's call: 'I Paul, the prisoner of Christ Jesus, for the sake of you Gentiles' (3:1).

The reference to him being a prisoner highlights the fact that he was literally in prison as he was writing, and that this was due to his higher calling as a 'prisoner of Christ Jesus.' He was in prison because of his commitment to Christ, and especially his commitment to proclaiming the gospel to the Gentiles, which had aroused the fierce opposition of some of his fellow Jews (see Acts 21:17–36; Rom. 15:14–32). In other words, Paul's assignment was hugely important (it came from Christ), and was hugely costly (he was in prison). So, too, our calling is very important, because it *comes from Christ Himself*, and it can be costly, even if it may not mean imprisonment!

Second, the assignment came from grace and was empowered by grace: 'the administration of God's grace that was given to me'. The word 'administration', which could be better translated 'stewardship', introduces the important concept of us being God's stewards or managers. This is so important to understanding our life purpose. It contains the idea that God is the owner, and that He has given us a particular entrustment that we are to manage. Moreover, this stewardship is something that we have received by God's grace. This is another dimension of grace. This grace goes beyond the saving grace that we have already discussed, to talk about the grace that is given in terms of serving and ministry.

Third, the assignment was for the sake of others. This was highlighted twice. In verse 1, Paul emphasises that he was a prisoner of Christ, 'for the sake of you Gentiles' and in verse 2, that his calling was 'for you'. For us too, it is important to be aware that God has gifted us for His service and that service concerns helping others.

Although there is no doubting that Paul's calling was special, let's be clear that the New Testament highlights that God has graced or gifted *every one of His people*. A few examples will suffice: 'We have different gifts, according to the grace given to each of us' (Rom. 12:6); 'Now to each one the manifestation of the Spirit is given for the common good' (1 Cor. 12:7); 'God has given each of you a gift from his great variety of spiritual gifts. Use them well to serve one another.' (1 Pet. 4:10, NLT). Notice each of us have received grace gifts from God and that they are to be used for the benefit of *others*.

REFLECT AND RESPOND

- **Take time to thank God that He has gifted you for a specific purpose. Pray that you might become a faithful steward of that life calling.**

MEMORY VERSE

'I became a servant of this gospel by the gift of God's grace given me through the working of his power.'

EPHESIANS 3:7

UNIQUELY GIFTED BY GOD

'Surely you have heard about the administration of God's grace that was given to me for you, that is, the mystery made known to me by revelation, as I have already written briefly. In reading this, then, you will be able to understand my insight into the mystery of Christ, which was not made known to people in other generations as it has now been revealed by the Spirit to God's holy apostles and prophets. This mystery is that through the gospel, the Gentiles are heirs together with Israel, members together of one body, and sharers together in the promise in Christ Jesus.'

EPHESIANS 3:2–6

As I mentioned yesterday, knowing one's specific calling is both tremendously important and hugely liberating. While we all have a general call as Christians, we don't all have the same specific call, and we don't all have the same gifts. Knowing what we are uniquely gifted for is essential if we are to be successful in fulfilling God's calling on our lives.

Paul was very clear what he was uniquely gifted for. He knew not only that God had called him, and that he was called to be an apostle of Christ Jesus, but he also knew the specific nature of his assignment. Here, in a re-emphasis of Ephesians 2:11–22, he highlights once again that his calling concerned the revelation that the Gentiles were included together with Israel in God's purposes. The idea of the Gentiles being blessed by God goes right back to Abraham (see Gen. 12:1–2), but the specific way that this would happen was revealed to and through Paul (see Eph. 3:6). It was not enough to know that he was an apostle, but that he was an apostle *to the Gentiles*, and given a specific message to bring to them. In contrast, Peter, also an apostle, was clearly called to be an apostle to the Jews (see Gal. 2:7–8).

This issue of knowing specifically what God has called us to is crucial and applies not just to specially commissioned apostles like Paul or those called primarily to serve in church leadership. Rather, I believe that God wants all of His people to get clarity on how they are to serve Him – in and through the home, the workplace and the local church.

So the question is, *how* do we know what we are specifically called to? There are three main ways. The first is through *revelation*! This was the way that Paul received and knew His call. I remember years ago, when I was still a fairly new Christian, sitting in a church service and suddenly sensing that the Lord was calling me to be a school teacher. Although this was only a temporary call, it encouraged me to step into teaching for a few years; first part-time during my postgraduate years and then full-time during our early years in Peterborough.

The second way that we can know our calling is through *consultation*. We are not always best equipped to discern our own gifts, hence we need other people, especially trusted mentors or church leaders. In addition, it is possible to get help from various personality tests and profiling. These can be generally helpful and give us a broad sense of how we best operate, but they are unlikely on their own to show us specifically how God has gifted us. Here again, we usually need others to accurately help us interpret these properly.

The third way that we can discern our calling is through *experimentation*: through life experience, trial and error. In my own case, I would say that this – along with revelation – has been by far the most helpful. For example, it took several years of pastoring a local church before I started to recognise that I had a gift of leadership. I had never been told that I had that gift, and at the time didn't know anything about personality testing. But as the church started to grow and we started to experience God's blessing, it became apparent to me that God had called me with a gift of leadership, as mentioned by Paul in Romans 12:8. This was later confirmed by doing personality profiles like DISC and Myers-Briggs.

So, don't worry if you haven't found your particular niche yet and don't sit around simply waiting and wondering. You could be there for a long time! Instead, get on the front foot and simply start serving where there are needs and opportunities. As you do, God will guide you, and others will help you discern where you are best suited for the long-term.

REFLECT AND RESPOND

- **Ask God to show you in what ways He has gifted you. Also ask a mature Christian, perhaps one of your leaders, to help you discern this.**

- **Start seeking opportunities to serve within your local church.**

- **Consider, too, how your gifts can be used in your workplace.**

MEMORY VERSE

'I became a servant of this gospel by the gift of God's grace given me through the working of his power.'
EPHESIANS 3:7

HUMBLE YET POWERFUL

'I became a servant of this gospel by the gift of God's grace given me through the working of his power. Although I am less than the least of all the Lord's people, this grace was given me' **EPHESIANS 3:7–8**

What makes a truly great leader? In his book *Good to Great*, Jim Collins describes what he calls a 'Level 5' or top-level leader. He and his research team examined why certain great companies seemed to outstrip comparative companies in the same field. When it came to looking at the type of leaders that led these most successful companies, they made a surprising discovery. Whereas many of the comparison companies were led by typically larger than life, very charismatic leaders, who they deemed to be 'Level 4' leaders', most of the stellar companies were led by what could be described as very unassuming 'Level 5' leaders. These 'Level 5' leaders managed to blend the paradoxical combination of deep personal humility with intense professional will. In other words they knew that the company was more important than them, and that they would do anything to help the company succeed. In summary, we could say they were humble yet powerful.[22]

This combination of humility and power is very evident in the ministry of the apostle Paul, two millennia earlier. On the one hand, notice his obvious humility. He knows that the gospel is bigger and far more important than himself, describing himself as its servant. In so doing, he was imitating the greatest servant of all, Jesus Christ, who although He was in very nature God, chose to leave heaven and 'made himself nothing, taking the very nature of a servant, being made in human likeness. And being found in appearance as a man, he humbled himself and became obedient to death – even death on a cross' (Phil. 2:7–8).

Not only does Paul call himself a servant, but he unselfconsciously calls himself 'less than the least of all the Lord's people'. Now, this is not a false humility, but rather is a genuine expression of the way Paul saw himself. Some commentators have suggested that he is emphasising that his name in Latin means 'small'. It also seems likely that he was small in stature physically. But here Paul is talking about more than this. In the words of John Stott, he may have been saying something along these lines: '"I am little … little by name, little in stature, and morally and spiritually littler than the littlest of all Christians." By affirming this he is neither indulging in hypocrisy nor grovelling in self-depreciation. He means it. He is deeply conscious both of his own unworthiness because he formerly blasphemed and persecuted and insulted Jesus Christ, and of Christ's overflowing mercy towards him.'[23] Yet Paul's humility is not just due to his awareness of his own past unworthiness, but because he knew that his apostolic ministry was not something that he deserved but was something given to him, 'by the gift of God's grace given me through the working of his power'. He was so conscious that all he had was a gift from God that he re-emphasises that his ministry was a 'grace' that had been given to him.

This double emphasis on grace, repeating what in effect he had said in 3:2 concerning 'the administration of God's grace', highlights that Paul was deeply conscious that not only his salvation but his whole ministry as an apostle was due to the grace of God. This was a key to his evident humility in ministry, and also was a source of his confidence and boldness. From the outset, when he simply announces himself as 'an apostle of Christ Jesus by the will of God' (1:1), through to this personal passage in 3:1–13, and throughout the rest of the letter, Paul is humble, but also very clear and very bold about his calling. The very fact that his assignment comes from God, and not from himself, is the key to his confidence. It's what makes him not just a humble leader but a powerful one, too.

This combination of being humble, yet powerful, is a great example for us all. It comes from knowing who we were without Christ, as well realising that through His amazing grace, He has gifted us to make a difference in other people's lives, for the glory of God.

REFLECT AND RESPOND

- **Consider whether you most need to grow in humility or in confidence concerning the call of God on your life.**

- **Ask God, through His grace, to help you grow in being humble yet powerful.**

MEMORY VERSE

'I became a servant of this gospel by the gift of God's grace given me through the working of his power.'

EPHESIANS 3:7

A SERVANT
OF THE GOSPEL

'I became a servant of this gospel by the gift of God's grace given me through the working of his power. Although I am less than the least of the Lord's people, this grace was given me: to preach to the Gentiles the boundless riches of Christ, and to make plain to everyone the administration of the mystery, which for ages past was kept hidden in God, who created all things.' **EPHESIANS 3:7–9**

As soon as I became a Christian, I had a passion to share the good news. I was quite bold, but not very sensitive and would tell people about Jesus – on trains, in the streets, on buses, on the doors – whether they wanted to hear the news or not! I still have that same desire to tell others, but hopefully have added a bit more wisdom and sensitivity to the way I do so!

This call to share the good news was clearly at the very centre of Paul's life mission, describing himself as 'a servant of the gospel'. As we have already seen (Day 37 – Eph. 3:6), this specifically concerned the good news that the Gentiles were now included in God's salvation purposes in Christ. Although Paul had a specific apostolic calling, his givenness to the gospel presents us with a great example in our own witness for Christ.

The question is, how are we present to the good news in a way that is both biblical and effective in our twenty-first century world? I find particularly helpful the 'BLESS' initiative developed by Dave Ferguson, Lead Pastor of Community Christian Church in Chicago, based on God's call to Abraham to bless him and make him a blessing (Gen. 12:2). As the spiritual descendants of Abraham in Christ (see Gal. 3), we are called to a similar mission. Based on this simple acrostic, B.L.E.S.S., let me share with you five missional practices you can apply in your life on a daily basis.

B – Begin in prayer. I like to call prayer for people who are not yet Christians, 'magnifying glass' prayers. As a boy, my friends and I would sometimes get a magnifying glass, place it in line with the sun, and focus the ray on a classmate's neck. Let's just say that this exercise helped us get a strong reaction as the sun's rays were intensified on that particular spot! In the same way, when we start to pray for people who aren't Christians, we can help focus the love and power of God into their lives. So why not draw up a list of people you know, who don't know Christ, and start praying for them. Then pray for yourself this powerful prayer: 'Lord, who do you want to bless through me?' and watch what He will do.

L – Listen. Rather than jumping in to speak, sometimes we have to learn to listen. By listening, we find out where people are and at the same time we can listen to the Holy Spirit and see how He would have us bless that person or community.

E – Eat. Jesus spent much time eating with 'sinners', and, especially in that Middle Eastern context, it was a way of showing love and acceptance to those around. You may not feel you have a strong enough bridge to start with a meal, but why not have a coffee or a drink instead? Alternatively, you could take the opportunity to eat together, along with others from your church.

S – Serve. Once again, we have the example of Jesus. In Acts 10:38 we see how Jesus 'went around doing good and healing all'. In the same way, we can serve people in practical ways by doing good works. We live in a culture where this kind of serving with acts of kindness is a simple and effective way of blessing people and showing them God's love. But let's also be open to serving others by offering healing to them in Jesus' name. In Ephesus, for example, Paul majored on healing as part of his gospel ministry (see Acts 19:11–12).

S – Share the story. First, share *your* story. In Acts 22 we can see how Paul shared his story of how Jesus had changed him, using a simple three-step pattern concerning his life: before he came to Christ, how he came to Christ, and his life after he came to Christ. You can do the same. Why not write out a simple outline of your story and be open to the Spirit's promptings to share what God has done for you. Then, get ready to share *His* story and be prepared to bring people to events where they can hear the good news.

REFLECT AND RESPOND

- **May I encourage you today to surrender or re-surrender your life to Christ, and offer yourself as a servant to the gospel.**

- **Start looking for opportunities to bless others and watch what God will do!**

MEMORY VERSE

'I became a servant of this gospel by the gift of God's grace given me through the working of his power.'
EPHESIANS 3:7

DAY 40

CALLED TO SERVE THE CHURCH

'His intent was that now, through the church, the manifold wisdom of God should be made known to the rulers and authorities in the heavenly realms'
EPHESIANS 3:10

Abraham Lincoln reportedly once said, 'If all the people who fell asleep in church on Sunday morning were laid out end to end … they would be a great deal more comfortable.' While amusing, this sadly reflects many people's negative stereotypes of 'church' today. Here in 3:10, Paul presents a very different vision of the Church. It is 'through the church', this company of converted, called-out Jews and Gentiles, that the 'manifold' or 'many-coloured' wisdom of God will be 'made known to the rulers and authorities in the heavenly realms'. The great Bible teacher and pastor John Stott put it this way: 'The church as a multi-racial, multi-cultural community is like a beautiful tapestry. Its members come from a wide range of colourful backgrounds. No other human community resembles it. Its diversity and harmony are unique. It's is God's new society. And the many-coloured fellowship of the church is a reflection of the many-coloured … wisdom of God.'[24]

This vision of the Church should deeply affect our attitudes and shape how we consider the investment of our time, talents and treasure. In recent years there has been a very helpful and healthy re-emphasis on the calling of God's people to serve Him in the workplace.

Given that most Christians spend a large proportion of their time there or at home, this is certainly important. Indeed, Paul, in the later chapters of Ephesians, teaches on the importance of living out our faith in the family and at work (4:28, 5:21–6:9). But he doesn't start there. Rather, the whole emphasis of chapters 1–3 and much of chapters 4–5 is on what he considers the most important sphere, which is the Church. Just as it is important to rightly equip people and be equipped for ministry in the world, equally, in the light of Ephesians, it is vital that God's people are equipped for ministry in the church. In 4:7, for example, Paul highlights that 'to each one of us grace has been given as Christ apportioned it'. This is clearly in the context of the church, as is 4:11, where he focuses on the fact that the ascended Christ gave gifts to people, including the leadership equipping gifts of apostles, prophets, evangelists, pastors and teachers. The purpose of these leadership ministries is not to do the ministry and exclude everyone else. Rather, they are gifted 'to equip his people for works of service, so that the body of Christ may be built up' (4:12). This is hugely important. Notice here that all of God's people are to be equipped for works of service. What are these? Certainly, they would include serving in the home and in the workplace, but the specific context here is that they are to serve *in* and *through* the Church.

A recovery of a vision for the local church and for our calling to serve in and through the local church is vital. Listen to these passionate words from Bill Hybels, senior pastor of Willow Creek Community Church: 'There is nothing like the local church when it's working right. Its beauty is indescribable, its power is breathtaking, its potential is unlimited … I believe the local church is the hope of the world. I believe to the core of my being that local church leaders have the potential to be the most influential force on Planet Earth. If they "get it", and get on with it, churches can become the redemptive centers that Jesus intended them to be. Dynamic teaching, creative worship, deep community, effective evangelism, and joyful service will combine to renew the hearts and minds of seekers and believers alike, strengthen families, transform communities, and change the world.' [25]

If we work together like this, in and through the local church, we can indeed change the world.

REFLECT AND RESPOND

- **What is your view of the local church? Do you need to get God's vision?**

- **Are you serving in and through the local church? If not, then take action to start getting involved.**

MEMORY VERSE

'I became a servant of this gospel by the gift of God's grace given me through the working of his power.'

EPHESIANS 3:7

CALLED TO SERVE GOD'S ETERNAL PURPOSE

'according to his eternal purpose which he accomplished in Christ Jesus our Lord.' **EPHESIANS 3:11**

It's so important to take the long view of life. In a society of instant gratification – instant meals, messaging, cash, loans – there is a huge danger of short-termism. God, on the other hand, takes the long view, in fact the 'eternal' view, and here Paul encourages us to take a similar perspective. In verse 10 we saw that God's 'intent was that now, through the church, the manifold wisdom of God should be made known to the rulers and authorities in the heavenly realms'. Here in verse 11 he highlights the fact that this was 'according to his *eternal purpose* that he accomplished in Christ' (my emphasis).

There's an old story about Christopher Wren, one of the greatest of English architects, who walked one day unrecognised among the men who were at work upon the building of St Paul's Cathedral in London, which he had designed. 'What are you doing?' he inquired of one of the workmen, and the man replied, 'I am cutting a piece of stone'. As he went on he put the same question to another man, and the man replied, 'I am earning five shillings, twopence a day'. And to a third man he addressed the same inquiry and the man answered, 'I am helping Christopher Wren build a beautiful cathedral'. That man had vision. He could see beyond the cutting of the stone, beyond the earning of his daily wage, to the creation of a work of art – the building of a great cathedral.

God's building of His Church is of far greater significance than the construction of a physical cathedral. Rather than a building with bricks and mortar, He is building a spiritual temple with the living stones of His redeemed people, so that He can live amongst and fill them with His glorious presence (see 2:20–22). This wonderful purpose was eternal. In the words of one commentator, Peter O'Brien, 'Just as in the eulogy of 1:3–14 God's choosing men and women in Christ to be his inheritance was in accordance with his eternal plan (1:11), so here also what has been made know through the church to the powers can be traced back to his everlasting purpose.'[26] Moreover, what He planned for before the creation of the world (1:4–5), was paid for in and through Christ and His cross (1:7–8; 2:14–18), and will be perfected when Christ comes back (1:9–10).

So, be encouraged. When you play your part in serving the local church, which is part of God's universal Church and part of His eternal plan, you are involved in something that is of *huge* and *lasting* significance. There is something deeply fulfilling about giving your life for something that really matters. One of the reasons I immediately felt a new sense of purpose when I became a Christian was because God's eternal Spirit came into my life, and I therefore became connected to His eternal purposes. And so did you, if you are in Christ!

That's why it's worth giving our very best to God and to the health and growth of the Church, because we are involved in the most purposeful activity available to mankind. This is brought out superbly in 1 Corinthians 15, in what is the classic chapter on the resurrection. Having gone to considerable lengths to teach how we are going to be physically resurrected with Christ on His return, Paul ends the whole chapter in the most practical way possible: 'Always give yourselves fully to the work of the Lord, because you know that your labour in the Lord is not in vain' (1 Cor. 15:58). I often find myself encouraged by this eternal perspective. Paul is saying in effect: in the light of your future resurrection, know that your labour now, in this body, and in this life, is not in vain. So give yourselves fully to His service. What an encouragement to give our very best to God and His purposes!

REFLECT AND RESPOND

- **Let me encourage you, again. If you are not serving God, find somewhere you can get involved and get going! If you used to serve, then get started again.**

- **If you are serving, then determine to continue to serve faithfully and enthusiastically.**

MEMORY VERSE

'I became a servant of this gospel by the gift of God's grace given me through the working of his power.'

EPHESIANS 3:7

SUFFERING AND GLORY

'In him and through faith in him we may approach God with freedom and confidence. I ask you, therefore, not to be discouraged because of my sufferings for you, which are your glory.'

EPHESIANS 3:12–13

One of my favourite films of the 1970s is *Rocky*. Rocky Balboa, played by Sylvester Stallone, is a small-time boxer who gets a rare chance to fight the heavy weight champion, Apollo Creed. His goal is simply to go the distance, so he puts himself through a demanding fitness regime, which includes eating raw eggs for breakfast and pushing himself through the pain barrier of extreme physical training. The outcome is that although Creed wins the fight by a split decision, it was the first time an opponent has lasted the full fifteen rounds against him. In the follow-up, *Rocky II*, Rocky goes on to win the re-match to become heavyweight champion of the world.

While I am not commending boxing per se (it's just a film!), there is a principle of training and paying the price that is common to most top sports. What is true in sport is generally true in life. If we are pursuing anything worthwhile, there will be both a price to pay and rewards to be received. This is certainly the case when it comes to giving our lives for the greatest cause of all, the eternal purposes of God. Here in these concluding verses to this section, Paul once again refers to his sufferings. Let me remind you that he was writing from prison (3:1), and throughout his ministry had suffered much to further the cause of Christ – spiritually, physically and emotionally. Yet he almost seems to make light of these sufferings, encouraging his readers not to be discouraged by what he is going through!

Today, in many parts of the world, people are still suffering much for the gospel, including enduring imprisonment, torture and even death. So how does this issue of suffering for the greater cause apply to the Western world, where the suffering for the gospel is much less obvious? I don't think we are supposed to wish for suffering and outright persecution, but we are called to give our best for His cause and that involves a cost. I find it helpful to try to focus the issue of the cost by considering three main ways that we can give ourselves for His glory, and that is by the use of our time, talents and treasure.

First, there is the issue of our time. Time is one of our most precious commodities, particularly in today's world when there seems so much pressure. Let me ask a few questions. Is Jesus Lord of your time? Are you honouring Him in your personal time by reading the Bible and in prayer? Are you meeting regularly with other Christians in the context of the local church? Are you giving of your time to share the good news with those who aren't Christians?

Second, there is the question of talents. God has gifted you. Are you using your talents for His glory – within your workplace, your home and the local church? (See Days 36–37.)

Third, there is the whole area of our treasure. This is often the most challenging. Jesus Himself taught much on the subject of money and possessions, and that what we do with our money is a key test of where our allegiance really lies. Are you putting God first in your finances – in tithes, in offerings and in good stewardship?

If, like Paul, we are truly aware of God's grace and call, and are fully grateful for our salvation, we will willingly give ourselves to Him even when it costs us. Here in verse 13, Paul makes it clear that he knew his sufferings were not in vain, but for the glory of the Gentiles who he had been called to reach. For us, too, we can give ourselves to the cause of Christ because we know that we are involved in the most important cause in the universe; which is to see other people's lives transformed for eternity. And as a result, we will be rewarded in eternity, in dimensions and ways that will make the rewards of top sportsmen seem entirely trivial and completely insignificant.

We will never regret the price we had to pay!

REFLECT AND RESPOND

- **Take time today to carefully and prayerfully consider how you can serve God more wholeheartedly, especially through the use of your time, talents and treasure. It will all be worth it!**

MEMORY VERSE

'I became a servant of this gospel by the gift of God's grace given me through the working of his power.'

EPHESIANS 3:7

WEEK 6 ACTION STEPS

1. Go to Day 50, Section 3, 'Purpose' and apply these truths to your own life.

2. Think about, pray about and share with your small group, ways you could serve God more effectively in and through your local church. If you are not part of a serving team, sign up this week. If you are already serving, ask God if and in what ways you could increase your involvement in His purposes, either in your existing area or in new ways.

REFLECTION

Jot down anything that particularly spoke to you this week and anything you have discovered about your identity, belonging and purpose.

PRAYER

Is there anything you would like to thank God for or ask Him for? If you want, write your prayer down here. This can be a good way of being able to look back and see what God has done.

PRAY FOR POWER

'For this reason I kneel before the Father, from whom his whole family in heaven and on earth derives its name. I pray that out of his glorious riches he may strengthen you with power through his Spirit in your inner being, so that Christ may dwell in your hearts through faith. And I pray that you, being rooted and established in love, may have power, together with all the saints, to grasp how wide and long and high and deep is the love of Christ, and to know this love that surpasses knowledge – that you may be filled to the measure of all the fullness of God. Now to him who is able to do immeasurably more than all we ask or imagine, according to his power that is at work within us, to him be glory in the church and in Christ Jesus throughout all generations, for ever and ever! Amen.'

EPHESIANS 3:14–21 (NIV 1984)

MAKE PRAYER
A PRIORITY

'For this reason I kneel before the Father, from whom his whole family in heaven and on earth derives its name.' **EPHESIANS 3:14–15 (NIV 1984)**

How important is prayer in your life? I remember as a young Christian pondering on why much of the present-day Western Church seemed relatively powerless. I compared our current situation first to historic revivals. Having had the privilege of spending many years studying George Whitefield, one of the leaders of the eighteenth-century 'Great Awakening', it became obvious to me that at the heart of this wonderful revival, as with other revivals in history, was its huge emphasis on prayer. I was also intrigued by why, even in our present-day, there seemed to be many powerful moves of God in non-Western cultures. Once again, I noticed a priority on prayer that was often missing in much of the better-resourced and relatively wealthy Western churches. So even as a young believer, I resolved to make prayer a priority in my life. Later, when we were involved in helping to start and lead a local church, establishing a culture of prayer was of critical importance.

One of the major reasons why prayer is so important is because it is the means by which God has ordained for us to *appropriate* what He has *already provided* for us in Christ. We have already seen this in Ephesians 1. Paul starts in 1:3–14 with a long declaration or hymn of praise for all that God has done for us in Christ, he then follows this up by praying for a *revelation* of this in 1:15–23. Here in 3:14–21 he prays again, this time building on the first prayer, but changing the emphasis to praying for an experiential *empowering*.

So what can we learn about prayer from this introduction to Paul's wonderful empowering prayer in Ephesians 3? First, that prayer flows out of a revelation of the truth. Paul's phrase, 'for this reason' highlights that he is praying because of what has been revealed. For us, too, our prayer flows best out of revelation. Which is why for centuries Christians have discovered that the best foundation for prayer is regular reading and reflecting on Scripture under the guidance of the Holy Spirit. Listen to the practice of George Muller: 'The first thing I did … was to begin to meditate on the Word of God; searching, as it were, into every verse, to get blessing out of it; not for the sake of public ministry of the Word; not for the sake of preaching on what I had meditated upon; but for the sake of obtaining food for my own soul. The result I have found to be almost invariably this, that after a very few minutes my soul has been led to confession, or to thanksgiving, or to intercession, or to supplication; so that though I did not, as it were, give myself to prayer, but to meditation, yet it turned almost immediately more or less into prayer.'[27] Let's learn from this example: feed on the Word, and let prayer abound!

Second, prayer is to be reverent and passionate. Interestingly, Paul mentions that he was praying in a posture of kneeling. Remember that he was in prison, so presumably he wasn't kneeling for reasons of comfort! However, this was different to the normal Jewish way, where people prayed standing up. Without getting locked in to the importance of postures of prayer – walking, standing, kneeling, lying prostrate and even on one's bed are all commended in the Bible – there is something significant here. The fact that Paul is kneeling suggests both a reverence – a position of submission before God – and a passion or intensity.

Third, prayer is to the Father. This is something that we looked at in detail on Day 16, but it is worth re-emphasising because Paul re-emphasises it. It's as if it's not enough for him just to say that he is praying – since all devout Jews prayed – but rather that he is praying 'before the Father'. This is a privilege that we get to enjoy in and through Jesus Christ, and we must never forget that we are not praying to the air, or babbling away, but are praying to a God who is our Father (see Matt. 6:5–15).

All of this highlights the priority and privilege of prayer.

REFLECT AND RESPOND

- **May I encourage you to take time to pray Ephesians 3:14–21 out loud, both for yourself and for others in your small group and local church.**

MEMORY VERSE

'Now to him who is able to do immeasurably more than all we ask or imagine, according to his power that is at work within us, to him be glory in the church and in Christ Jesus throughout all generations, for ever and ever! Amen.'

EPHESIANS 3:20–21

PRAY FOR THE STRENGTHENING OF THE SPIRIT

'I pray that out of his glorious riches he may strengthen you with power through his Spirit in your inner being' **EPHESIANS 3:16**

I don't know about you, but I regularly need to be spiritually strengthened. One particular instance comes to mind. I was due to speak at a Bible conference in North Wales. For some particular reason I felt a sense of spiritual heaviness, and knew that I needed God to help and strengthen me before preaching. So I went down to the beach and started praying in tongues as the Holy Spirit enabled me. I soon found myself praying deeply and loudly, all the time very aware that the Spirit was doing His work. After about half an hour of praying, I suddenly felt the heaviness lift, and a new joy and peace come to me. I turned around, went back down the beach, this time skipping over the pools and rejoicing in my new-found strength. That evening I preached, and what a time we had!

I am sure that there are times when you, too, feel spiritually weak, and you become aware that you need strength to walk in God's ways, to please Him, and to resist the influences of temptation and evil. The good news is that not only is strength freely available, but God wants to release that strength to you and to your fellow believers, as you pray 'that out of his glorious riches he may strengthen you with power through his Spirit in your inner being'.

Remember that Paul was writing to believers in Ephesus and the surrounding region, who had formerly been subject to spiritual powers that had enslaved them and would have still been very much aware of the battle in the heavenly places (see 6:10–20). Having already prayed in 1:17–20 that God might give them a *revelation* of His mighty power and strength already at work in them, Paul now goes a step further and prays for an actual *manifestation* of that power. It's one thing to have the power of God potentially available to us, it is another to actually live and walk in it. That's why we need to pray!

First, we are praying to a Father who is both willing and able to meet our need for spiritual strength. As with 1:17–18, where Paul is praying to the 'glorious Father' who has provided 'the riches of his glorious inheritance' (see Days 16 and 19), so here in 3:16, Paul is keen to emphasise that God will provide for His people 'out of his glorious riches'. Know this, that as you pray for yourselves and others, God is more than able (3:20) to answer out of His inexhaustible and wonderful resources.

Second, note that the Father will strengthen us in our 'inner being'. This highlights the important point that there is far more to us than just our physical bodies. There is an inward part of us, a spiritual dimension to our lives.

Third, he prays that we might be strengthened 'with power through his Spirit.' Once again, as with the prayer for 'the Spirit of wisdom and revelation' in 1:17, so here in this prayer for empowering, Paul is praying that the Spirit who already has come to us (1:13–14), will now make Himself known to us. This experiential dimension is so important to grasp. It is not enough to be the temple of God, and have God dwell in and amongst us (2:21–22), we need to pray that God will actually strengthen us 'with power'.

Finally, note that this is a *prayer*! Presumably, Paul believes that *as a result of his prayers* for them, the experience of the believers will be different. As a church leader I take this responsibility of praying for believers very seriously. But lest we think this is just something for leaders, Paul towards the close of this letter encourages *all* his readers to engage in prayer: 'And pray in the Spirit on all occasions with all kinds of prayers and requests. With this in mind, be alert and always keep on praying for all the Lord's people' (6:18). What kind of prayers can we pray for fellow Christians? Certainly the prayers found in chapters 1 and 3, these great prayers for revelation and strengthening.

REFLECT AND RESPOND

- **There's an ancient prayer that many find helpful to pray today, and it's simply this: 'Come, Holy Spirit '. So pray and ask God to strengthen you and those around you with power through His spirit.**

MEMORY VERSE

'Now to him who is able to do immeasurably more than all we ask or imagine, according to his power that is at work within us, to him be glory in the church and in Christ Jesus throughout all generations, for ever and ever! Amen.'
EPHESIANS 3:20–21

PRAY FOR THE INDWELLING OF CHRIST

'I pray that out of his glorious riches he may strengthen you with power through his Spirit in your inner being, so that Christ may dwell in your hearts through faith.' **EPHESIANS 3:16–17**

How much of Christ's presence do you know and enjoy on a daily basis? This is a key question. This is not to undermine your identity or sense of security in Christ, which Paul has gone to great lengths to establish in chapters 1–2. But here in Ephesians 3:17, Paul has moved on from celebrating our *position* in Christ to praying for our *experience* of Christ dwelling 'in our hearts through faith'.

This language of Christ dwelling in us carries the meaning of Him coming to live in us permanently. Let me illustrate. For the first eighteen years, KingsGate Peterborough met in many temporary venues. Eventually, after gathering in various schools and community centres, we moved into our purpose-built 'home', settled down in a different way and have been meeting there ever since. In a similar way, Paul's prayer that Christ may dwell in us contains the idea that Christ doesn't want to just visit us, but to live in us, and make His *permanent home* in us. Earlier in the letter, Paul has made it clear that we already have the Spirit since conversion (1:13–14), and in the parallel letter of Colossians this means that now we have Christ Himself in us (see Col. 1:27). But Paul is not praying for Christ to 'come into our hearts', in other words for us to *become* Christians. Rather, he is praying for those who are *already* Christians to know the permanent indwelling of Christ in a personal and experiential way.

This experiential indwelling is something that Christians throughout the ages have enjoyed, and something that we can enjoy today. Listen to the words of some of the great leaders of the eighteenth-century revival. This was the regular experience of George Whitefield: 'Oh, what sweet communion I had daily vouchsafed with God in prayer … How often have I been carried out beyond myself when sweetly meditating in the fields! How assuredly have I felt that Christ dwelt in me and I in Him! And how did I daily walk in the comforts of the Holy Ghost and was edified and refreshed in the multitude of peace.'[28] Or listen to John Wesley on his famous conversion: 'I felt my heart strangely warmed'.[29] Or his brother Charles Wesley: 'Thou, O Christ, art all I want. More than all in Thee I find'.[30] Or the Moravian, Count Zinzendorf: 'I have one passion; it is Christ, and Christ alone'.[31] Or the Welsh Calvinistic Methodist, Howell Harris: 'I felt suddenly my heart melting within me, like wax before the fire, with love to God my Saviour'.[32] Each of these men came from very different traditions and yet they all had this in common; an ongoing experience of and passion for the person and presence of Christ Himself.

The great news is that this dynamic and intimate experience of Christ is not just for great leaders but for *all believers*. The encouragement of this text is that we can follow Paul's example and pray this prayer for ourselves and for other Christians. As we do, we will know 'sweet communion' with Christ in a way that not only will wonderfully touch our emotions, but will lead to us becoming more like Him (see Eph. 4:24; 5:1; Rom. 8:29; Gal. 5:22–23). Let me close by quoting again from the twentieth-century preacher Martyn Lloyd-Jones as he applies this prayer to our lives: 'So you begin to pray, and you go on praying in faith until some marvellous moment comes and suddenly you find yourself knowing Christ. He will have manifested Himself to you. He will have taken up His abode in you, and settled down in your heart.'[33]

REFLECT AND RESPOND

- **Set aside some extra time to seek God today, and pray that through the Spirit you will have a new experience of Christ dwelling in you. Pray this same prayer for other believers in your small group and local church.**

MEMORY VERSE

'Now to him who is able to do immeasurably more than all we ask or imagine, according to his power that is at work within us, to him be glory in the church and in Christ Jesus throughout all generations, for ever and ever! Amen.'

EPHESIANS 3:20–21

PRAY TO KNOW THE POWER OF HIS LOVE

'And I pray that you, rooted and established in love, may have power, together with all the saints, to grasp how wide and long and high and deep is the love of Christ, and to know this love that surpasses knowledge' **EPHESIANS 3:17–19 (NIV 1984)**

Our KingsGate mission statement is 'Transforming lives … by the power of God's love.' This is not just a slogan. We have seen thousands of people's lives changed as they have understood and experienced the transformational power of God's love. This love is the *agape* love of God, different and greater than all other kinds of love (see Day 23). It is the unconditional, unselfish love of God that heals us when we've been hurt or let down by false love or lust.

Paul of course knew this. Hence, having prayed for the strengthening of the Spirit and the indwelling of Christ, he continues to pray that believers might know this kind of love, once again referring to a powerful experience of love. Two pictures are used here to convey the same point.

First, there is the reference to being 'rooted … in love.' A friend of mine was walking with a friend of his who owned an orchard. He stopped and asked the owner: 'What makes healthy apples?'. The answer was of course: 'A healthy apple tree'. Fundamental to any healthy tree is that the roots go down deep into the right soil. This is the picture that Paul is using here: if we want our lives to be healthy, we have to put deep roots down in the soil of love.

Second, there is reference to being 'established in love'. Years ago, I heard a story of someone visiting a building site and noticing how long it was taking to dig the foundations. He queried one of the team on the need for such deep foundations, and received back the following answer: 'We are digging deep, because we are planning to build high.'

So what is this love? Some commentators have suggested that it's *our* love for God, for the Word of God and for others. But, going with the majority, I believe that this is referring to *God's* love for us in Christ. This is the soil that we need to be rooted in and the foundation that we need our lives to be built on. In practice, both our love and His love are vital but the order is important. Paul brings this out later in Ephesians 5:1–2: 'Follow God's example, therefore, as dearly loved children and live a life of love, just as Christ loved us and gave himself as a fragrant offering and sacrifice to God.' In other words, when we know that we are dearly loved children and we know how much Christ loved us *then* we can and will live a life of love.

Having prayed for the Ephesians that they might be rooted and established in love, he prayed that they might move on and grow in somehow comprehending the vastness of Christ's love. In doing so he uses four dimensions, each of which are worth pondering on.

First, think about the breadth of His love and how wide it is. If we think of God's love for the whole world, we can see that His love extends to all humanity – to every person, from every tribe and nation, from every background and culture. This love includes Jew and Gentile, male and female. It includes everyone. No one is outside the breadth of His love. Then think about how long His love is. This could refer to the eternal dimension of God's love. It includes a love that planned for us to be His children from before the creation of the world. It involves the decision to send Christ to save us, and a love that will never leave us for all eternity. Then think about how high His love is.

This is a love that not only reaches to the heavens, but catches us up in that love, by raising us up with Christ and seating us with Him in the heavenly places. Then think about how deep His love is, how He came down from heaven to earth and how he became a man and humbled Himself by dying on a cross for us.

REFLECT AND RESPOND

- **Take time to think about the wonder of God's love for you in Christ.**

- **Pray for yourself and others that you might be rooted and grounded in God's love, and that together you might begin to grasp the full extent of this love.**

MEMORY VERSE

'Now to him who is able to do immeasurably more than all we ask or imagine, according to his power that is at work within us, to him be glory in the church and in Christ Jesus throughout all generations, for ever and ever! Amen.'

EPHESIANS 3:20–21

DAY 47

PRAY TO BE FILLED WITH HIS FULLNESS

'that you may be filled to the measure of all the fullness of God.' **EPHESIANS 3:19**

Enthusiasm is attractive and contagious! If you meet someone who is enthusiastic about something it can often rub off on you. Similarly, if you go to a sporting, musical or dramatic event, the enthusiasm of a crowd or audience often spreads. It's the same when it comes to Christianity. Very often people come into church services filled with vibrant worshippers, and they are struck by the enthusiasm, but somehow sense that there is something more than the enthusiasm of an ordinary kind of crowd.

This is because there is something more! Unbeknown to many, the original meaning of the word 'enthusiasm' is 'inspired by a god'. Religious critics of Whitefield and the eighteenth-century revivalists often criticised them for their 'enthusiasm'. But actually they were referring to something very positive! Whitefield and his fellow revivalists had a true enthusiasm in the sense that they were filled not with 'a god' but with the presence of the One true God. Rather than being a bad thing, this is what Paul prays for at the climax of this empowering prayer in Ephesians 3!

In fact, I would go as far as to say that an absence of this enthusiasm, or being filled with the presence of God, is often the major reason why the Church declines. Contrastingly, where people are filled with God's fullness, the Church is revived.

I have used this illustration over the years when teaching on the Holy Spirit. I take a glass and start filling it with water. Part-way through, I ask whether the glass is full, and of course the answer is 'no'. Then I pour until the water reaches the brim, and then go to someone in the congregation – usually someone I know well – and keep on pouring so that the water spills over and they get wet! I then talk about the importance of us being so filled with God's presence that we overflow, so that others get wet!

What does it mean for us to be filled in this way? It's important to note that theologians make a distinction between the incommunicable and communicable attributes of God. The incommunicable attributes refer to those characteristics of God that He alone possesses, such as being omnipresent, omniscient, omnipotent and eternal. The communicable attributes are characteristics of God that, by grace, He shares with His redeemed children, such as holiness, righteousness and the fruit of the Spirit, listed in Galatians 5:22–23. So, back to this prayer: as we are strengthened by the Spirit of God and indwelled by Christ, we can and will be increasingly 'filled to … all the fullness' of the communicable attributes of God, such as love, joy, peace and holiness.

In addition to the fruit of the Spirit, the more we are filled with God's presence, the more we can begin to exercise the gifts of the Spirit, as listed for example in 1 Corinthians 12:7–11. Interestingly, we see in Acts 19, when Paul first arrived at Ephesus, that the first thing he does is to ensure that the twelve disciples are filled with the Spirit (see Day 14). Having discovered that these disciples of John the Baptist haven't even heard of the Holy Spirit, he baptises them into the name of the Lord Jesus and then lays hands on them. We read how: 'When Paul placed his hands on them, the Holy Spirit came on them and they spoke in tongues and prophesied' (Acts 19:6). There is some debate as to whether this is the kind of experience that Paul is referring to in Ephesians 1:13, when he talks about the believers receiving the seal of the Spirit. But whatever the case, Paul clearly expected that Christians would receive the Spirit in this way: with some kind of experiential overflow that included spiritual gifts.

It's so important that we position ourselves to receive this initial infilling of the Spirit. But it is also important that we follow Paul's exhortation to 'be filled with the Spirit' (5:18) in an ongoing way. Paul's prayer here in Ephesians 3:19, may well include this initial infilling, but it surely goes beyond that, to speak of an ongoing lifestyle of fullness and of being continually filled.

REFLECT AND RESPOND

- **Pray for yourself and for others – for the initial and ongoing filling of the Spirit. Pray this, believing that you can be filled to the measure of all the fullness of God!**

MEMORY VERSE

'Now to him who is able to do immeasurably more than all we ask or imagine, according to his power that is at work within us, to him be glory in the church and in Christ Jesus throughout all generations, for ever and ever! Amen.'

EPHESIANS 3:20–21

PRAY WITH EXPECTANCY

'Now to him who is able to do immeasurably more than all we ask or imagine, according to his power that is at work within us' **EPHESIANS 3:20**

It's good to be reminded that praying to a God who is 'able to do immeasurably more than all we ask or imagine'. Listen to this description of prayer: 'Now let the full glory of the scene in heaven dawn on you. In human pictorial terms, Jesus is seated on the throne, on the right hand side of the Father. You, sharing the throne of Jesus in the Spirit, are seated beside Him. When you intercede according to the will of God, aided by the Holy Spirit indwelling you (who intercedes for you and through you), you turn to Jesus and make your plea for His glory and for His sake. By your authority 'in Christ' you hand the request to Jesus. He joins His almighty intercession with yours and turns to the Father to present your united intercession (Jesus and yours!) and then seals it by saying His royal "Amen", being in his very essence your enthroned "amen". Because of who Jesus is, because of what He accomplished at Calvary, He agrees with you in prayer; He is the sovereign "Amen" of your prayer.'[34]

I love the way that God answers our prayers, and often does so in ways that are much more than we were asking or imagining. This is certainly the case when it came to our request for land and a church building in Peterborough. Having looked at various potential sites we settled on six acres in an industrial area. Although it would have worked, and we spent considerable time praying, researching and going to planning, we eventually failed to get planning permission by a 4–3 vote. To cut a long story short, despite the disappointment, we were led to a different site – this time 12.4 acres – not only double the original, but in a much better location. The Lord opened the door of favour for us within the city council, and we received the support of both the sitting MP and the opposition candidate. We went through the planning process again and this time won on a 9–0 vote. We were able to build a stunning 83,000-square-foot building and still have over seven acres left for future plans. Many times, my wife, Karen, and I pinch ourselves and ask: How did this happen? It happened because we have a God who overruled, and gave us *immeasurably more* than we were asking or imagining.

I use this illustration to make a point. But here in Ephesians 3:20, Paul's focus is on something greater that concerns the *internal* work of God in our lives and the lives of His people. Having prayed for the Spirit's strengthening, Christ's indwelling and love and God's fullness, He concludes here by giving glory to 'him who is able to do immeasurably more than all we ask or imagine, according to his power that is at work within us'. Notice that his concern is God's power *within us*. What is that power? It is, as we have already seen, the same power that raised Christ from the dead and seated Him to His right hand, far above all principalities and opposing forces (see Day 21).

I love the way the full weight of this is brought out more fully in the Amplified Bible's translation: God 'is able to [carry out His purpose and] do superabundantly, far over and above all that we [dare] ask or think [infinitely beyond our highest prayers, desires, thoughts, hopes, or dreams]'.

This is so amazing that's it's worth pausing on each phrase at a time.

- God is able to do what we ask
- God is able to do all that we ask
- God is able to do all that we ask or imagine
- God is able to do more than all that we ask or imagine
- God is able to do much more than all we ask or imagine
- God is able to do immeasurably more than all we ask or imagine

In the light of this, we can be assured that as we pray, God is greater than any problem we face. He is greater than any sin, greater than any sickness, greater than any strife, and greater than any obstacle that we face, either in our lives or in the lives of those around us.

REFLECT AND RESPOND

- **Re-read and declare the 'God is able' statements from today. Then pray!**

MEMORY VERSE

'Now to him who is able to do immeasurably more than all we ask or imagine, according to his power that is at work within us, to him be glory in the church and in Christ Jesus throughout all generations, for ever and ever! Amen.'

EPHESIANS 3:20–21

PRAY, GIVING HIM ALL THE GLORY

'to him be glory in the church and in Christ Jesus throughout all generations, for ever and ever! Amen.'
EPHESIANS 3:21

If you have ever been overawed by a stunning painting, poem or play, and silently thanked the painter, the poet or the playwright, you were in some way giving glory to the creator of that work. In the same way, we as God's people are to live in such a way that our whole lives are giving glory to God, who is both the One who created us, and re-created us in Christ.

This is the point that Paul is making here at the close of this prayer and the close of this stunning first half of his letter to the Ephesians. The ultimate goal of all that He said in these three chapters, and the end result of his prayers being answered, is that glory goes to God. This takes us right back to Ephesians 1:3, where Paul starts the whole letter by blessing God the Father for having blessed us with every spiritual blessing in Christ. Throughout 1:3–14, Paul frequently reminds his hearers why God has so blessed us: it is ultimately not just for our good (although it certainly is for our good), but it is 'to the praise of his glorious grace' (1:6), and for 'the praise of his glory' (1:12,14).

Paul ends his prayer in Ephesians 3 by reminding his hearers that the goal of us being strengthened by the Spirit, indwelled by Christ, established in His love and filled with God's fullness, is that all the glory goes back to God! Moreover, this glory is something that will rebound to Him, not just in this life and in this age, but throughout all generations, forever and ever.

This is such a helpful reminder: that our salvation is ultimately not about us just being blessed, but about God Himself being glorified. This has been recognised throughout the ages. The highly influential Westminster Confession of Faith in 1646 stated that 'the chief end of man is to glorify God, and to enjoy Him forever'. If we are to glorify God, then we must enjoy Him, and be satisfied in Him. As we do so, it will ultimately be for our good and for His glory.

It is important to note that God is not just glorified through our individual lives, but 'in the church and in Christ Jesus'. Martyn Lloyd-Jones once again superbly unpacks the significance of this: 'Nothing gives such glory to God as the Christian Church. God manifested his power when He created the world out of nothing … The mountains, the rivers and the raging sea, lighting and thunder, all proclaim His glory … But there is nothing that so proclaims the glory of God as the Christian Church, the body of which Christ Himself is the Head. Nothing is so wonderful as the fact that men and women, such as you and I, men and women who were steeped and lost and dead in sin, should have become members of the Body of Christ. Here we have the mightiest display of the glory of God.'[35]

Finally, we must note that this glory goes to God 'throughout all generations' (that is in history), and 'for ever and ever' (that is in eternity). So, as we live the transformed life, not only will we be blessed, but God, our Creator and Redeemer, will receive the highest praise!

REFLECT AND RESPOND

- **Take time to reflect on the fact that the ultimate goal of living the transformed life is that God will receive the glory.**

MEMORY VERSE

'Now to him who is able to do immeasurably more than all we ask or imagine, according to his power that is at work within us, to him be glory in the church and in Christ Jesus throughout all generations, for ever and ever! Amen.'

EPHESIANS 3:20–21

WEEK 7 ACTION STEPS

1. Go to Day 50 and declare the 'prayer promises.'

2. Pray the wonderful prayer from Ephesians 3:16–19. Write the
   four verses on a piece of card or somewhere easy to access, such
   as on a phone. Use it to pray for yourself, your family, friends and
   members of your small group and church family. Watch what
   God will do!

REFLECTION

Jot down anything that particularly spoke to you this week and anything you have discovered about your identity, belonging and purpose.

PRAYER

Is there anything you would like to thank God for or ask Him for? If you want, write your prayer down here. This can be a good way of being able to look back and see what God has done.

SUMMARY

As we come to this final day, let me paint you a picture of the transformed life, and encourage you to start applying these truths to your life.

SECTION 1: IDENTITY

In answer to the 'Who am I?' question, declare these promises:
- In Christ I have a new identity (1:1)
- In Christ I am a saint (1:1)
- In Christ I am a recipient of grace and peace (1:2)
- In Christ I am blessed with all spiritual blessings (1:3)
- In Christ I have been chosen to be holy from before the foundation of the world (1:4)
- In Christ I have been predestined to be His child (1:5)
- In Christ I am highly favoured (1:6)
- In Christ I am redeemed (1:7)
- In Christ I am forgiven (1:7)
- In Christ I am expectant (1:9–10)
- In Christ I am sealed with the Spirit (1:13)
- In Christ I have the Spirit as a deposit of the future (1:14)
- In Christ I am greatly loved (2:4)
- In Christ I have come alive (2:5)
- In Christ I've been raised up and seated with Him in heavenly places (2:6)
- In Christ I am saved by grace through faith (2:8)
- In Christ I am God's workmanship (2:10)
- In Christ I am a new creation (2:10)

SECTION 2: BELONGING

In answer to the 'Where do I belong?' question, declare these promises:

- In Christ I belong to the family of God (1:1–2)
- In Christ I am included in the people of God (1:13)
- In Christ I am part of His body (1:23)
- In Christ I have been brought near to God (2:13)
- In Christ I am part of a new race (2:15)
- In Christ I have access to the Father by the Spirit (2:18)
- In Christ I am a fellow citizen with God's people (2:19)
- In Christ I am a member of God's household (2:19)
- In Christ I am a part of His holy temple (2:21)
- In Christ I am part of His dwelling place (2:22)

SECTION 3: PURPOSE

In answer to the 'What am I living for?' question, declare these truths:

- In Christ I have a new purpose in God (1:1)
- In Christ I am to live for the praise of His glory (1:6,12,14)
- In Christ I have works that God has planned in advance for me to do (2:10)
- In Christ I have an assignment from God (3:1–2)
- In Christ I have been uniquely gifted by God (3:2–6)
- In Christ I can be humble and powerful (3:7)
- In Christ I am a servant of the gospel (3:7–8)
- In Christ I am called to serve the Church (3:10)
- In Christ I am called to serve God's eternal purpose (3:11)
- In Christ I am called to suffering and glory (3:13)

SECTION 4: PRAYER

Declare these wonderful prayer promises:

- In Christ I can pray to the Father (1:17; 3:14)
- In Christ I can pray for the Spirit of wisdom and revelation (1:17)
- In Christ I can pray to know God better (1:17)
- In Christ I can pray to be enlightened (1:18)
- In Christ I can pray to know the hope of his calling (1:18)
- In Christ I can pray to know the riches of his inheritance (1:18)
- In Christ I can pray to know the greatness of his power (1:19–20)
- In Christ I can pray to a gloriously rich Father (3:14)
- In Christ I can pray for the strengthening of the Spirit (3:16)
- In Christ I can pray to know the indwelling of His presence(3:17)
- In Christ I can pray to be rooted and established in love (3:17)
- In Christ I can pray to know the dimensions of His love (3:18–19)
- In Christ I can pray to be filled to the fullness of God (3:19)
- In Christ I can pray knowing that God is able to do immeasurably more than all I ask or imagine (3:20)
- In Christ I can pray knowing that all the glory goes to Him, for ever and ever! (3:21)

I so hope that this has helped you receive a revelation of your new identity, place of belonging and purpose in Christ. May you be eternally transformed.

Endnotes

[1] C.E. Arnold, *Ephesians: Exegetical Commentary on the New Testament* (Grand Rapids: Zondervan, 2010).

[2] P.T. O'Brien, *The Letter to the Ephesians* (Cambridge: Eerdmans, 1999).

[3] Information from the annual *REVEAL* survey by the Willow Creek Association.

[4] D. Tunningley, *Unreachable* (Lancaster: Sovereign World, 2001).

[5] P. Yancey, *What's So Amazing about Grace?* (Grand Rapids: Zondervan, 2002), p45.

[6] B. Pascal, *Pensées* (London: Penguin Books, 1995).

[7] J.I. Packer, *Knowing God* (London: Hodder & Stoughton, 1993).

[8] J. Ritchie, *Five Hundred Gospel Sermon Illustrations* (Grand Rapids: Kregel Publications, 1987).

[9] V. Frankl, *Man's Search for Meaning*, originally published in 1946.

[10] J. Nye, Homeless millionaire found dead before he could be told about his fortune: Body of 'heir' to 300 million discovered frozen to death under railway bridge, *Daily Mail*, 30 December 2012.

[11] K. Lowrie, *Chilean miner speaks at DBU chapel*, 28 March 2012, accessed April 2015 at www5.dbu.edu/news/campus-news/419/

[12] J. H. Dubbs, *Leaders of the Reformation*, originally published in 1898.

[13] G.F.L. Konig, *The Life of Martin Luther, the German Reformer, in Fifty Pictures*, originally published in 1853, accessed April 2015 at archive.org/details/lifeofmartinluth00kn/

[14] D.M. Lloyd-Jones, *God's Way of Reconciliation: An Exposition of Ephesians 2* (Grand Rapids: Baker Books, 1998), p143.

[15] W. Churchill, *Their Finest Hour*, Vol. 2 (Boston: Houghton Mifflin Harcourt, 1986), p103.

[16] M. Luther, *Concerning Christian Liberty*, originally published in 1520, accessed April 2015 at www.gutenberg.org/files/1911/1911-h/1911-h.htm/

[17] C.S. Lewis, 'The Inner Ring', in *They Asked for a Paper: Papers and Addresses* (London: Geoffrey Bles, 1962), p142.

[18] P.A. Taylor, *Ephesians: God's Eternal Glory* (Maitland: Xulon Press, 2007).

[19] Lloyd-Jones, *God's Way of Reconciliation*, pp381–392.

[20] R. Warren, *The Purpose Driven Life: What on Earth Am I Here For?* (Grand Rapids: Zondervan, 2012).

21   N.T. Wright, *Paul and the Faithfulness of God* (London: SPCK, 2013), p355.

22   J. Collins, *Good to Great* (London: Collins Business, 2001).

23   J.R.W. Stott, *The Message of Ephesians: God's New Society* (Leicester: Inter-Varsity Press, 1979), p119.

24   Ibid, p123.

25   B. Hybels, *Courageous Leadership* (Grand Rapids: Zondervan, 2002), p23.

26   O'Brien, *The Letter to the Ephesians*, p248.

27   G. Muller, *The Autobiography of George Muller* (New Kensington: Whitaker House, 1984).

28   G. Whitefield, *George Whitefield's Journals* (Edinburgh: Banner of Truth, 1978), p61.

29   J. Wesley, *John Wesley's Journal* (Chicago: Moody Press, 1951) accessed May 2015 from http://www.ccel.org/ccel/wesley/journal

30   C. Wesley, 'Jesus, Lover of my Soul', in *Hymns and Sacred Poems*, originally published in 1740.

31   Cited in D.M. Lloyd-Jones, *Unsearchable Riches of Christ: An Exposition of Ephesians 3* (Grand Rapids: Baker Books, 1979), p162.

32   H. Harris, *A Brief Account of the Life of Howell Harris, Esq.*, originally published in 1791, available online from Google Books.

33   Lloyd-Jones, *Unsearchable Riches of Christ*, p152.

34   W. Duewel, *Touch the World through Prayer* (Grand Rapids: Zondervan, 1986), p43.

35   Lloyd-Jones, *Unsearchable Riches of Christ*, p314.

Further Reading
On Ephesians

Arnold, C.E., *Ephesians: Power and Magic: The Concept of Power in Ephesians in Light of Its Historical Setting* (Cambridge: Cambridge University Press, 1989).

Arnold, C.E., *Ephesians: Exegetical Commentary on the New Testament* (Grand Rapids: Zondervan, 2010).

Hoehner, H.W., *Ephesians: An Exegetical Commentary* (Grand Rapids: Baker, 2002).

Lincoln, A.T., 'Ephesians', in *Word Biblical Commentary*, Vol. 42 (Dallas: Word, 1990).

Lloyd-Jones, D.M., *God's Ultimate Purpose: An Exposition of Ephesians 1* (Edinburgh: Banner of Truth, 1978).

Lloyd-Jones, D.M., *God's Way of Reconciliation: An Exposition of Ephesians 2* (Edinburgh: Banner of Truth, 1972).

Lloyd-Jones, D.M., *The Unsearchable Riches of Christ: An Exposition of Ephesians 3* (Edinburgh: Banner of Truth, 1979).

O'Brien, P.T., *The Letter to the Ephesians* (Grand Rapids: Eerdmans, 1999).

Snodgrass, K., *Ephesians: The NIV Application Commentary* (Grand Rapids: Zondervan, 1996).

Stott, J.R.W., *The Message of Ephesians: God's New Society* (Leicester: Inter-Varsity Press, 1979).

Virgo, T., *Does the Future have a Church?* (Eastbourne: Kingsway, 2003).

Wright, N.T., *Paul for Everyone: The Prison Letters – Ephesians, Philippians, Colossians and Philemon* (London: SPCK, 2002).

Other Recommended Works

Calvin, J., *Institutes of the Christian Religion*, originally published in 1536.

Carson, D.A., *A Call to Spiritual Reformation: Priorities from Paul and His Prayers* (Grand Rapids: Baker Books, 1992).

Dallimore, A.A., *George Whitefield: The Life and Times of the Great Evangelist of the Eighteenth-Century Revival*, 2 vols (Edinburgh: Banner of Truth, 1970, 1980).

Fee, G.D., *God's Empowering Presence: The Holy Spirit in the Letters of Paul* (Peabody: Hendrickson, 1994).

Hawkins, G.L. and Parkinson, C., *Follow Me* (South Barrington: Willow Creek Association, 2008).

Langmead, C., *Robber of the Cruel Streets: The Prayerful Life of George Muller* (Farnham: CWR, 2006).

Piper, J., *Desiring God* (Colorado Springs: Multnomah, 1986).

Sheets, D., *Intercessory Prayer* (Ventura: Regal, 1996).

Urquhart, C., *In Christ Jesus* (London: Hodder & Stoughton, 1981).

Virgo, T., *God's Lavish Grace* (Oxford: Lion Hudson, 2004).

The Transformed Life church programme comes with FREE online sermon outlines for leaders and videos for your small group.

Same subject

Grow together as your whole church explores true identity, belonging and purpose through Ephesians 1–3.

Same time

Transformed Life can be used at any time of the year. Using the available resources, you can prepare and explore together as a whole church or in your small groups.

All ages

As well as this 50-day devotional for adults, activity books for early and primary years are available for purchase. Free resources for youth are available online.

A 7-week church programme for **all** ages

What to do next

Sign up

All the resources and information you need are available on the *Transformed Life* website. You can register at **www.transformed-life.info** for a welcome pack and to receive more information.

Invite

Once you have decided to take part, invite the rest of your church to join in. As there are resources available for all ages, the whole church can be involved in the programme together.

Bulk orders

This 50-day devotional is designed to underpin the whole programme. To order bulk copies for your church or small group, visit **www.cwr.org.uk/transformedlife**

smallGroup central

All of our small group ideas and resources in one place.

Small Group Central is packed with clear, easy to use inspiration for your small group. On this website, you will find:

- **Free teaching:** Andy Peck, a CWR tutor, has created videos on the practicalities of leading a small group

- **Free tools:** templates, discussion starters, icebreakers – all you need to lead a group study effectively

- **Resources:** books, booklets and DVDs on an extensive list of themes, Bible books and life issues.

Log on and find out more at
www.smallgroupcentral.org.uk

|COVER_{TO}|
cover

vital:

Life EVERY DAY

SMALL GROUP
ToolBox

Every Day with Jesus

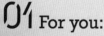